for the children of Gaza

Edited by Mathew D. Staunton & Rethabile Masilo

The Onslaught Press

Published in Oxford by The Onslaught Press
11 Ridley Road, OX4 2QJ
July, 2014

ISBN-13 978-0-9927238-4-2

Typeset in Le Monde Livre & Le Monde Sans,
& designed by Mathew D. Staunton

Printed by LightningSource.

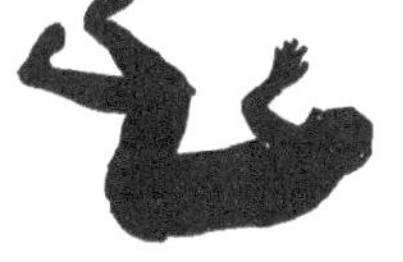

contents

preface

Operation Protective Edge, described by US Secretary of State John Kerry as "Israel's appropriate and legitimate effort to defend itself" from Hamas rocketeers and tunnel builders, is now in its fourth week. Unfortunately for the civilian population of Gaza, however, there is little in this operation that could reasonably be considered defensive. The destruction of Gaza's civilian infrastructure and its only power station, the targeting of schools, hospitals, mosques, fishing boats, orchards, and the beach is more about making life intolerable for Gazans than it is about ending rocket attacks. The civilian death toll, and the number of child casualties in particular, make it difficult to see this as anything other than collective punishment. And yet we are asked every day to believe that these casualties are 'legitimate', 'unavoidable', 'appropriate', 'justified', 'necessary', and 'reasonable' and that children are dying because they are being used as 'human shields'.

Suffering is increasingly mediated by diplomats, official spokespeople, broadcasters, news corporations, community leaders, spin doctors, and legal teams, but usually with no more than a passing commentary. We see more and more pictures of dead children on our screens and in our newspapers but the texts and speeches that accompany them are full of ambiguous and misleading words, or words with no meaning at all. Sometimes there are so many dead children that it is more expedient to forget about words altogether and simply use numbers.

The contributors to this book are telling the story of our anger and disgust and horror. You will not be surprised to discover that there is darkness in many of the texts that follow. But there is also joy and beauty. Its aim is much less to accuse than to paint a correct picture of what most of the world seemingly does not see, or chooses not to see, and we think that a right recognition of the reality of Gaza today needs to be accompanied by the right remedial action. Such action is in the hands of all of us, even if the leaders of the world, who are indeed in the best position to act, do not.

What is at stake in Gaza goes well beyond the politics of sides and enters the consideration of crime and of killing. There are many accomplices on both sides and as in any crime, they, too, must be held accountable. Bishop Tutu has said that "*if you are neutral in situations of injustice, you have chosen the side of the oppressor. If an elephant has its foot on the tail of a mouse and you say that you are neutral, the mouse will not appreciate your neutrality.*" The work presented here by many artists and writers from all corners of the world attempts, unlike the non-actions of those who actually have political clout and power, to choose the side of the oppressed.

Suddenly, in the face of these killings, it does not matter that tunnels have been dug, or that rockets are being launched at Israeli cities. Even if you are right, what suddenly matters is choosing to kill your opponent, who is weaker.

Mathew D. Staunton & Rethabile Masilo

My dogs are sleeping in the shade. I inherited them, Just like I inherited my government.

I am good to them. Quiet. They sleep and get fat. I didn't give them ridiculous names or make their lives about me. I once knew an artist who had two cats called Gilbert and George and a poet with a dog called Bukowski. They could neither paint nor write.

My dogs are sleeping in the shade

They are lazy bastards. They sleep and get fatter, only stirring when other dogs come snuffling round the back yard.

My dogs are sleeping in the shade.

I inherited them just like my government.

Oliver Lomax

Ach Abairse an Focal agus Leigheasfar Sinn

Uaireanta
Creidim i gcumhacht mhór na bhfocal
Chun ord a chur ar mo smaointe,
Chun eagar a chur ar mo bhraithstintí,
Chun tonn tuile an neamhchomhfheasa
A choinneáil faoi smacht.

Uaireanta,
Go h-áirithe in amanta na cinniúna
Nuair a thiteann gach lúb ar lár
Agus nuair a scaoiltear le gach olc
Ó chófra Phandóra
Ar chinn na bpáistí óga,
Faighim deacair a chreidiúint puinn ina gcumhacht.

Ach anois díreach
In ainneoin an éadóchais a thiteann
Mar diúracháin ón spéir
Glacaim misneach is meanma
As feachtas beag seo bhur gcuimhneacháin,
As feachtas beag seo ár n-agóide,
As cumhacht bheag ár bhfocal is ár liníochta.

Suím anseo i mo ghairdín cúil
Agus scríobhaim focail neamhchumhachta
Ar pháipéar bán
Nár cheart a bheith bánaithe seasc
Chun ainmhí fiáin na feirge
A scaoileadh soar ó m'instinní.

Ní thuigim an duine daonna,
A dhrochmhianta
Nó fadhb mhór an oilc—
Mothaím an féar tais
Faoi mo chosa lomnochta
Agus i dtromluí mo dhúiseachta
Braithim bhur bhfuil,
A pháistí soineanta na Pailistíne
Ag fliuchach méaracha mo chos.

Má tá cumhacht
Sna focail fhánacha seo,
Má tá ord nó eagar iontu,
Fiú aon fhiúntas faoi leith,
Táid tiomnaithe daoibhse,
A pháistí neamhurchóideacha caillte,
Scriosta, ár lean,
Ag ollphéisteanna an Náisiúnachais.

Tim Quinlan

But only say the Word and We shall be Healed

Sometimes
I believe in the great power of words
To order my thoughts,
To keep my feelings in line,
To stanch the tidal flood
From the great unconscious.

Sometimes,
Especially in these fatalistic times,
When every stitch is dropped
And every evil released
From Pandora's Box
Right on top of children's heads,
I find it hard to believe in their power at all.

But right now
Despite the despair that rains
Like missiles from the air
I take courage and hope
From this little campaign to remember you,
From this little campaign of protest,
From the little power of our words and drawings.

And so I sit here in my back garden
And write impotent words
On blank paper
That should neither be barren or bare
So that the wild animal of my anger
May be released from within.

I do not understand human beings,
Their shoddy desires
Or the great mystery of evil
And I feel the dampness of the grass
Beneath my naked feet
And in this waking nightmare
I feel your blood,
Children of Palestine,
Wetting my feet.

If there is any power
In these stray words,
If there is order and form in them,
Or even some worth
They are dedicated to you,
Innocent lost children,
Destroyed, alas
By the monsters of Nationalism.

Tim Quinlan

Child of Moments

He runs
along the shoreline
sand between his toes
his mother knows
this dancing.

He runs
imagining himself bird
imagining the air
free on his rising feathers
joy in his eyes.

He runs
instead, so swiftly ended
into the bullets that fly
from the enemy
blood runs, blood runs.

Anna Husain

Shield of trust II

“We know how it happens, what
it is: intifada is a series of marbles
on rooftops, hard-knocking them
into shape, though there are still
no stones on domes that gild
the heights of Jerusalem, no stones
where the seeds of history sleep.”
It is raining fire on Gaza now
and I chase men in and out of holes
the way boys hunted field rats
in the hills of Lesotho when earth
was young. They will keep between
now and forever the memory
of their death. I have snuffed out
all candles for their night must darken.
Like a snake I have heat vision eyes.
Let them grope in obscurity, suffer
the pain of millions as I did. I might
just keep the neck of a young child
in a choke-hold to make him die.
He is Eric Garner. There is no *why*
to that, the question that remains
on tongues of people has become
what for. The one single answer
to a *where* question is *there*, there
upon land that is considered holy.

But please do not accomplice me
with apartheid, even at its worst,
where police beat kids up and killed
some alive, do not underrate
my just concern. I am mightier
for continuing to use my force
to start wars and finish them off.
I have no mouth to talk, no alms
to offer. I cut off a terrorist's arms
with my faith, for I am Tzahal.
And so I sayeth unto thee, hear me
and fear me, for I have no qualms
about nothing. No qualms at all.

Why it matters

So also, when you see these things taking place,
you know that the kingdom of God is near. Luke 21:31

This is why it matters earth is dying—
birds fly north, one leading by the beak of its mouth
the tired and the hungry from the south,
no chance to perch on the ruin below—sometimes
when they're tired they fall out of the sky like stones
of manna given to the Israelites when they were hungry
and the desert refused to help, giving neither fruit
nor game. Still, birds mostly fly, unwilling to land
but for brief stops, before continuing on,
afraid of nature that kills them. Along the way,
white bears float on blocks of ice, bury
themselves and hibernate in their camouflage
of retreat, safe from the warming heat,
and sail in search of boys and girls
who hold them and give them gentle names.
This is why it matters what is dying. The same
cannot be said about what is already dead.
Peace is dying, and neither to the south
nor to the north, east or west, can the victim
go. He is that bear on a piece of ice
drifting from the lands of god. It matters
for all the reasons a peacemaker must stand
in the line of fire and take shirt off, shoes
and blood-soaked djellaba, to expose a body
whose scars move to a centre that grows
like rivers going back to their mutual spring.

The statue of Richard

Sand is after you,
the hands of dunes
are starting to shift
up the legs and arse
of your white dress;
on the way from a land
of doom where law
belongs to one man
and one man alone,
people stop to ply
the fat strings
of your heart—
as many as twenty
home-made bombs
in Baghdad yesterday
alone. So much
sand is in your veins
that the world is true,
ready to leave the room
you used to water-board
men in, man-of-stone.

for Dick (16 April 2013)

Two

27 July, 2014

They come from around the world
following the smell of gunpowder, and news
another family has gone down. Down
as a nation goes that was hiding behind
Jericho walls. One after another its bricks
waste. They pray they will get there in time,
for the toil that awaits. The younger ones
have only heard about war from stories told.
And they never believed half of them.
But the smell of death reaches their noses
and piques their resolve, tugs at their guts.
Trucks converge at a certain point and roll out
together toward Babylon. From America, too,
more board Boeings after furtive training periods
and head for Israel. The mating call
of bombs strong, rotting flesh waiting
to greet them.

And there is sound that finds ears,
that reminds us of what in South Africa,
during the era of truth and reconciliation,
a former army sergeant told everyone there
he discovered—in the bush at night when no one
was around but his troops and a few kaffirs—
that the part of the human body slowest to burn
is the buttock. Two groups from neither country
will meet at the junction of Israel and Gaza, a thousand
which CNN says are leaving America today,
and untold numbers of others from the Arab world.
As more bombs bleed over the walls that separate
two future neighbours, the wound of troops swells
at the borders of freedom and prepares to spill
pus on the way to a permanent, scabbed healing.

Rethabile Masilo

The night is long faced

The night is long faced,
accustomed as it is to misfortune,
every night the Palestinian,
under occupation, since 1948,
tries to sleep in its shadow.

It's people killed everyday,
children left as orphans,
daily it is hit, in the face,
and in the guts,
again and again,
until this process,
starts to feel normal.

This is the taste of occupation,
people learning to live in fear everyday,
knowing that any minute, their front door,
could be kicked down, trying to stay human,
trying desperately to stay sane,
knowing that their children, mothers and fathers,
may never return home again.

The children are seen as terrorists ,
for simply using slingshots against tanks and drones,
the media likes to portray it as a terrorist state,
its people as the enemy,
while turning the bully,
into a victim.

In the mornings, seeds of bitterness spread,
as grim days stretch out this peoples agony,
and the longing for their liberation,
and though Palestine does not exist on the map,
it exists in the hearts of millions around the world.

Like the night, they have learnt,
that with warm buds of thirst,
freedom is existence, and existence is freedom,
and that one day, from the rivers to the sea ,
with hope on their sides, they will be free.

Dave Rendle

I want to be a princess

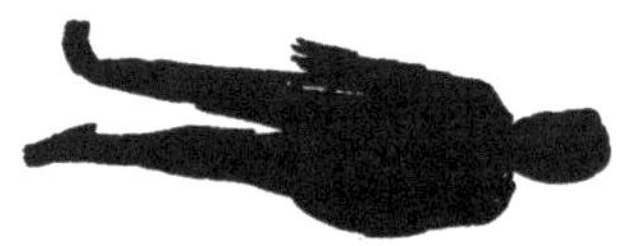

or a cat

or a monster who eats cats

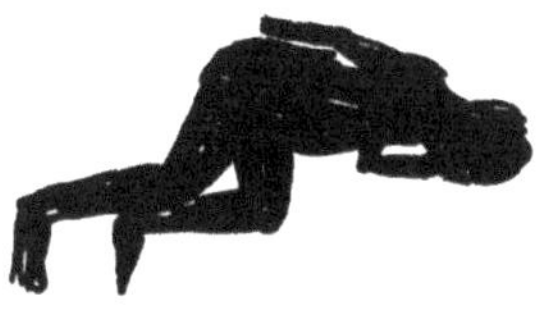

and dig a hole

and set a trap

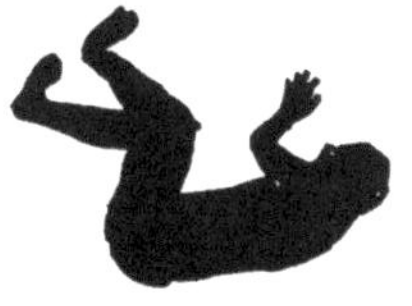

and fill your shoes with plastic people

fill my pockets with spare noses

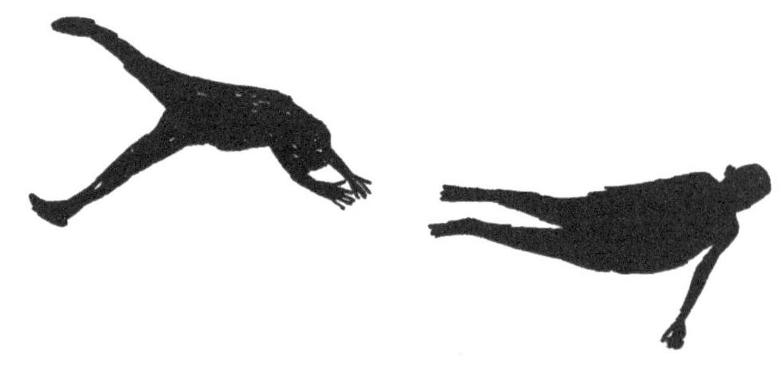

(little pebbles)

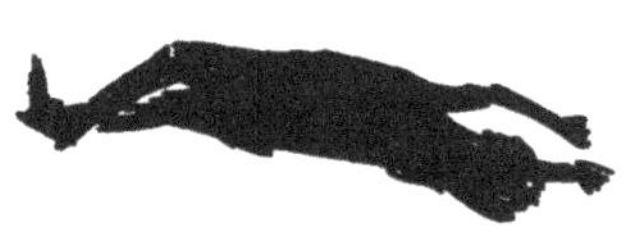

to replace the ones you steal

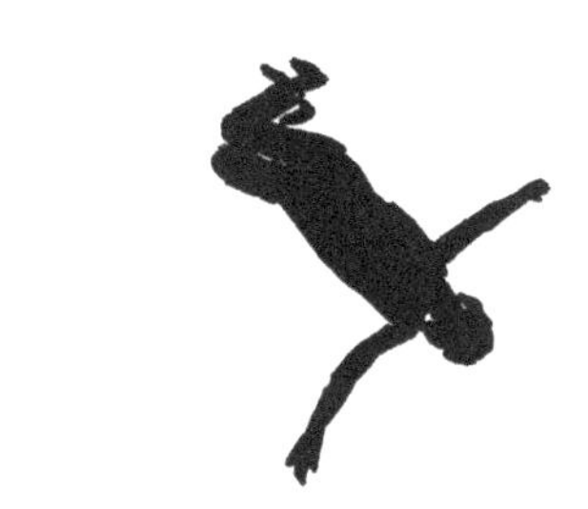

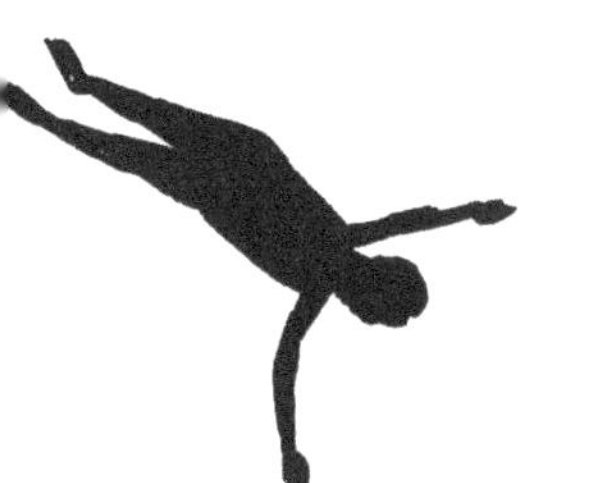

and climb a tree

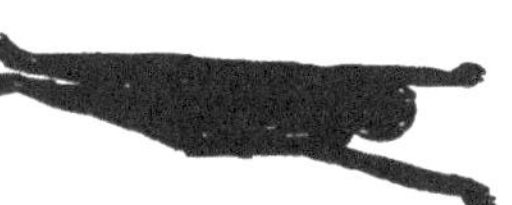

and run on sand

and be a princess

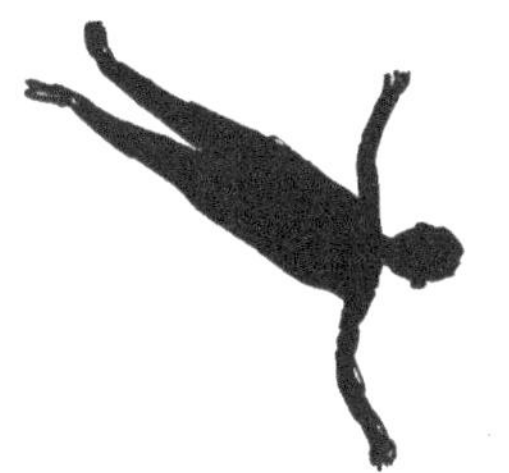

or a cat

The Israeli Occupation: Different Voices

Very recently I heard a young Israeli called Yehuda Shaul being interviewed on Radio Ulster. Yehuda is the co-founder of Breaking the Silence, an organization that aims to expose the harsh realities of the Occupation to fellow Israelis. His words made such a deep impression on me that I made up my mind to put my own thoughts on the Occupation into an essay for *Facts and Arts*. I made five attempts at writing the essay and each time abandoned it, defeated by the scale of what is happening in the occupied territories. But this morning I remembered that in 2010 I had written an unfinished novel a section of which touched on two opposing points of view, one Israeli and the other Palestinian. I found the relevant part and read it. Yes, I thought, this is probably as close as I will ever come to expressing the tragedy. Yet what I have written is fiction. What will I do? And then I remembered something the English philosopher Francis Bacon once wrote: "Truth is so hard to tell, it sometimes needs fiction to make it plausible."

So here is my fiction. Here is my truth.

They fettered his mouth with chains
And tied his hands to the rock of the dead.
They said: You're a murderer.
They took his food, his clothes and his banners,
And threw him into the well of the dead.
They said: You're a thief.
They threw him out of every port,
And took away his young beloved.
And then they said: You're a refugee.

Mahmoud Darwish (1941-2008), Palestinian poet

My name is Yohevet. I live in Area C on the West Bank. This is my home. International law says I am living here illegally but I spit on international law. I spit on Europe and I spit on American liberals. These cowards have the blood of millions of my race on their soft hands. I will tell you about my father. My father was born in Vilnius, Lithuania and every day he lived there he was reminded that he was a Jew. Once in the school playground some boys and girls wrestled off his pants and held his hands away from his body so that they could all see the sign of circumcision. The boys sneered and the girls sniggered. He was twelve years old when this happened.

In 1937 he and his parents moved to Warsaw. Two years later Hitler invaded Poland and announced that he intended killing every Jew living there. Rabbi Stephen Wise, head of the American Jewish Congress, went to see President Roosevelt and presented him with a large dossier, *Blueprint for Extermination*, which documented Hitler's plans. Roosevelt tut-tutted and straightaway went back to dealing with Japan's threat in the Pacific. For as far as Roosevelt was concerned territory was what mattered.

When Britain's House of Commons heard about the Rabbi's dossier it stood for a minute's silence. And as the honourable members stood with heads bowed Anthony Eden their foreign secretary made an eloquent speech in which he expressed the hope that Hitler would refrain from exterminating these unfortunate people.

For some reason Eden's hope and Roosevelt's disapproval did not stop the Austrian butcher and six and a half million Jews were murdered. One of them was my grandmother, taken from her home and raped by German soldiers. It was my father who found her next day hanging from a lamp-post. But here's what I couldn't understand when I was a child. Britain had declared war on Germany in order to save Poland. Hadn't they?

No. They had declared war to preserve the balance of power in Europe. That was the reason. They could have fought to evacuate European Jews to Palestine but no, this would have upset the Arab oil producers.

But now we are in the West Bank and this is our home, my father, my wife, my children and I. We are here and here we stay. The miracle is that he never lost his mind. I think the reason is that he has been able to let things out. He dreams at night about things that happened and the next day if he gets the chance he will talk to me about it. One incident comes back often in his sleep and up to now he has managed to wrench himself awake from it before the final part. He is searching the darkened streets of Warsaw trying to find his home. Everywhere he goes there are blackened remains of buildings and high walls that go on forever. He cannot get over the walls and he is not sure if his home is a ruin for with every ruin looking the same as the others there are no landmarks. As he looks around tearful and frightened a boy only a little older than himself approaches and asks him: "Where is your star?" and he answers: "I do not have a star. I am not a Jew", for that is what his parents have taught him to say to German soldiers. The boy strips him from the waist down and shines a torch on him. "There is your star," he says and it is when he forces my father to lie face down on the road that the dream ends.

There I will give her back her vineyards, and will make the Valley of Achor a door of hope. There she will respond as in the days of her youth, as in the day she came up out of Egypt. Hosea: 11:1

I dream. The night is strung with stars light years away. Foetid, sweet and thick is the smell from the sea. If people could see they would think it strange, a man like me, sitting here in the bay at such an hour so close to the slow surge of the tide. The waves are sluggish now with their cargo of human waste and the yellow foam fingers towards me. I almost faint with the weight of memories. Dreaming I feel the castles and the rock-pools in my hands and round the bend of the Mediterranean I touch the girl from Rafah. She is old now, or dead, old or dead it doesn't matter. But I am stealthy when I think of her for my wife is alive, and worse, she hears me in my sleep. Yet dreams will come. Dreams. What is it they call them? There are names for them. The sovereignty of the mind, the charming illusion. When your land has been taken and your home from in front of you and your son cut down and his wife imprisoned what do you have?

I tried to take their children for a walk this morning but the stench from the wrack and the reek of the sea turned us away. This is a place of death. Thirty-seven days ago a soldier blew off the crown of my brother's head. Samih, stubborn foolish Samih, took the short cut to bring us bags of peas. The short cut indeed. Yesterday they killed a boy of fifteen, armed they said, and today they shot a toddler who I'm told will never walk. But maybe that's wrong, maybe she will. Even in this enclosure it is still possible to exaggerate.

Sometimes I think we would be better without Hamas. America tells us we would. Europe tells us too. Sometimes I am almost sure they are right, other times I tell myself that without our representatives we would only have the peace of the pigsty. I remember the Aborigines, the Tibetans and the Burmese who live under the same sky as we do. They look up and they have dreams. Mandela had the wildest dreams of all and he looked up from his prison cell and took them. It's hard to credit, I didn't know it until yesterday that in America they still call him a terrorist. What a strange place America is. An angel, a girl from that very country, showed this very thing to me on her computer. Write to the House of Representatives, she told me, and you will see it is true. Enclose a postage-paid self-addressed envelope, she said, and they will write back and explain that they have him down as a terrorist and that he is subject to restricted movement. But all that comes from the time apartheid suited them and I'm sure they will fix it soon. An anomaly, she said.

When will they get round to us? The truth is, I would fly like the wind if they let me. Would I leave my wife and grandchildren? Yes. I do not love her and the children will be victimised with or without me. The woman is a fool. She sleeps with title deeds in a plastic bag under the pillow and keeps in her pocket the key to a house that isn't there. There are dreams but this is stupidity. And now I will tell you another truth. Nobody cares about us except the agitators for justice and the world says that they are left-wing cranks and troublemakers. All it takes to get into Palestine is to be born here. America and Israel blame us for this accident but still they will not let us leave. To get out we have to die because no matter how many times we say we are sorry for what the Germans did it will not be enough. Our jailers will never forgive us or allow us to forget the Holocaust.

What else must we answer for? Thirty million Indians were murdered by the British through famine and forced labour. India, we are sorry. Fifty million Chinese were murdered by Mao in the Great Leap Forward. China, we are sorry. In whose interest is it that we are so maligned? As for the suffering Jews who survived the Holocaust, I do not believe there are any of them here. For if there were they would speak out. The colonisers who are here in their place hold the handed down memory in their hearts like possessive lovers. But they hold us in their clenched fist. Their terror of their own extinction blinds them to our terror and to the memory of who did what. Allah forgive them for they know not what they do.

Colm Herron

Then What?

So you say the land is yours.
Then what?
So you put hundreds of thousands to flight.
Then what?
So you take over land.
Then what?
So you round up thousands.
Then what?
So you build a wall.
Then what?
So you bulldoze homes.
Then what?
So you drop bombs.
Then what?
So you invade.
Then what?
So you kill children.
Then what?
So you shell hospitals.
Then what?
So you say you won't talk to terrorists.
Then what?
So you say the land is yours. Then what?

Michael Rosen

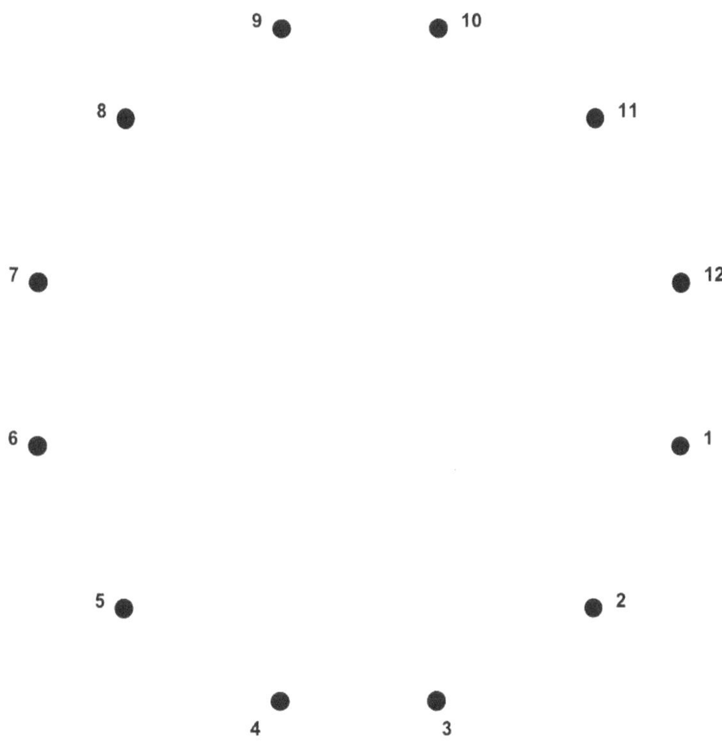
9
10
8
11
7
12
6
1
5
2
4
3

What Courage

To kill with a gun,
a grenade, poison gas,
a mortar, a missile,
a rocket, a rock stone,
a razor-edged knife?

To steal a child
and roast him
with his life
still insisting,
breath breathing
blood bursting
through veins?

His little brother
forces a finger
under his eyelids
looking for
love and laughter,
shadow puppets,
stories from rare
books and stupid
"I spy" games
that every day
shone there.

Who will these kids
bred up on blood,
barrages of gunfire,
bruises and battering,
no thing nor place
nor person safe,
for whom a stone's throw
does not mean
a short distance away
who will they grow
up to become?

What courage to suppose
that any culture, any faith
safely coopts its prophets,
angels and a holy God
to build a nation on
such slaughtered innocents?

Pamela Mordecai

Skinflint

At 2:40 his head is cleared
though he is dazed and bathed
in wrong noise, he cannot yet
open his eyes if the light is less
blinding than the earth.

At 3:18 he raises
his arm to wipe his eyes, still half
interned and bearing
soft clothes. This is not
birth: sorting the equivalences
is only one of our tasks.

I am waiting for his total emergence in pain
and press his form where no one has poured water.
Home is a grave and among the things
it buries is differentiations,
but he is not thinking of them his head
is full of broken images
that can't be sorted by the divas of sympathy.

He is not cute dogs that speak in baby languages.
He is not the NYT debate about whether poetry matters.
Skinflint and dizzy with cartridges
lions on a hypo
we take out our eyes
our virgin eyes
and put them on paper towels to dry.

The red route through
indifference is equivalence
the red route through
equivalence is distinction
the red route through
distinction is action.
The red route through
one house into another
is taken by giant robots
antennae popping like eyes
from their backs, for the *homestoi*
is the space of politics and my sitting
room can be a smoothed space,
as the sweet grass mowed.

So what if my son came up
through the water with his eyes
open. So what if he breathed
on the NHS and his cord
wrapped twice around his neck
was gently and silently slipped off
as I dug him up ferried him up

to graze and hear him
singing 'up above the world so high'
at 7:45. There are brands of noosing
for rubber necks can be snapped
if braced by inexpert love:
the first missiles knock
the second collapse
distinctions between storeys.

My other letter today was
to Meg Whitman
of Hewlett Packard and the board
of the USS. My other son was
trying to remember
who is parents were,
when the diamond fell the air
snuffed him into the loop
of his representative
his improbable survival.

Andrea Brady

Let us pretend

Let us pretend
that we haven't been this way before
too recently and too often
that this is the way forward
that it is the road to the peace
which eluded you when you sent
planes and tanks and men
into Lebanon, Ramallah, Jenin,
Gaza, Gaza, Gaza.

Let us pretend
that this time will be different
that this time will be worth it
that you can tot up the lives
of dead children and collateral families
and declare victory
that security can be measured
in flattened houses
burials and tears.

And let us pretend
that when you build settlements and walls
and criss-cross the country with roads
and stitch it with checkpoints
and cut down olive groves
and throw people from their homes
let us pretend then
that the only terrorism in town
is the anger of young men
who build rockets they can barely aim
who have no hope,
who see their homeland dismembered before them.

Let us pretend
that this tit for tat
this tit for bloody tat
is the only way
is the legacy you will leave
your children and your children's children
their children and their children's children

Let us pretend there can be no hope
that milk and honey cannot be shared
that Israeli and Palestinian can never
live together, laugh together, love together
two flags flutter together
let us press our face to the cross-hairs
and close our eyes
and stop up our ears
and still our beating hearts
and let us pretend, Bibi,

let us pretend.

Steve Pottinger

An Image from Gaza

He's calling to his children,
a wife, a mother. He's running
unaware his clothes and skin
have been torn by the blast. He crashes
to his knees, his eyes black holes.
Home and neighbour's houses
spread like rubbish tips.
He chokes, writhes, vomits
among rubble. Down the street,
on the roof of a building
that still remains, the dust clears.
A sniper takes aim.

Sally Flint

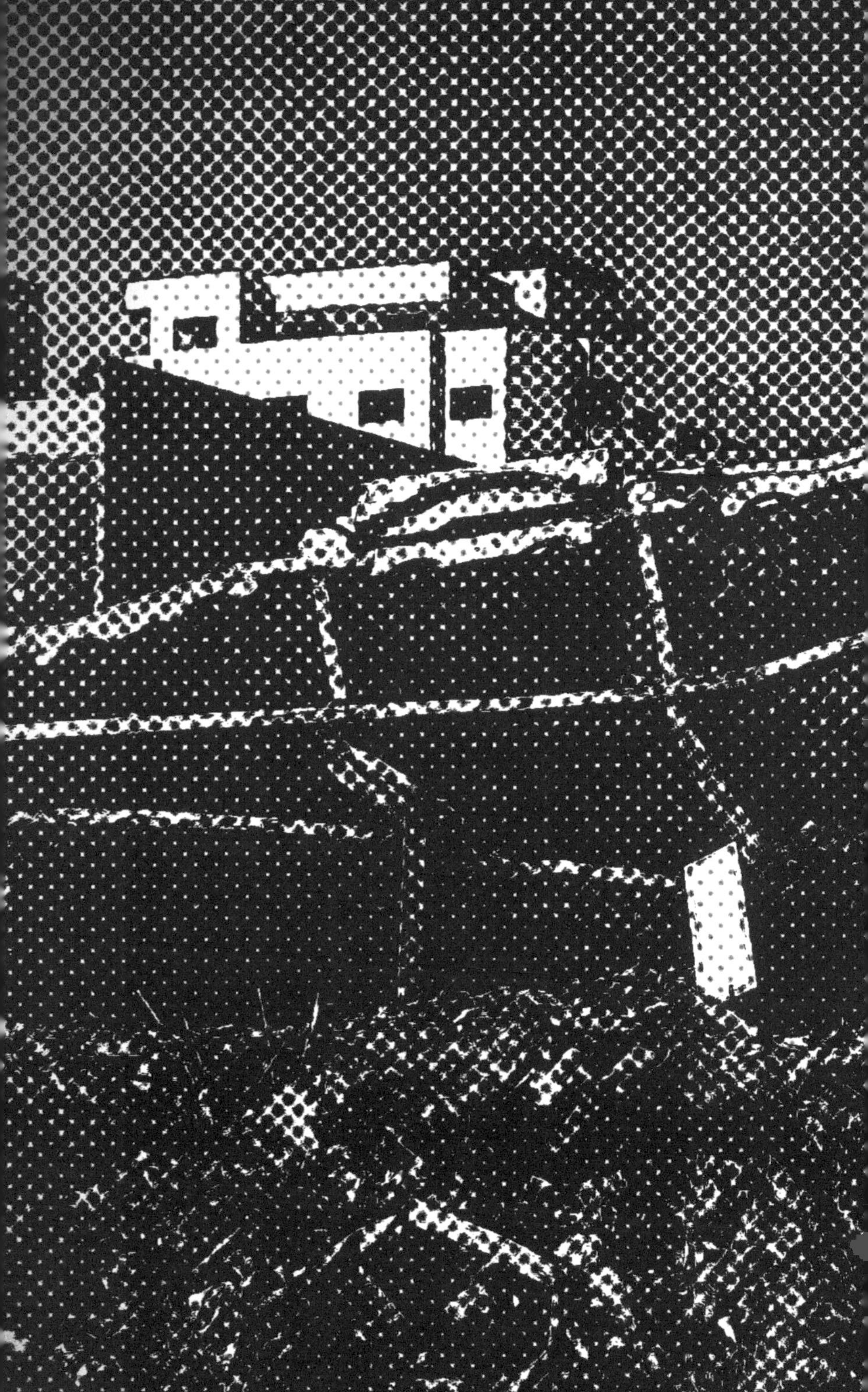

Open Door

Come in
My door is open
My windows clear
My welcome clean
Be you friend or stranger
The foe of ignorance
And dangerous myth
My table round
A circle for new comers
We break bread

I'll pour Italian espresso
You bring baclava from Beirut
We will muse over differences
Between olives
Big and small
Green and black
Let us chew on the options

You be the Muslim
I'll be the Jew
I'll poem a phrase
You sing a chorus
We shall dance in the telling light
For all to witness
We can
Know the grace of
Bird song
Wind chime
Morning star

The world reshaped
In two part harmony
One whole peace

I shall follow you
To your city
To your home
I carry flowers
A curious manner
A wish to learn
A want to know
A need to be

I will share your tastes
The aromas of your kitchen
The lay of your garden
The chatter of children
The photos you cherish
The souls past and present
They whom you carry
In the wellspring of your heart

An old man dies
A child is born
Years gone by
Days to come
Dreams deferred
Deeds to do
You tell me stories
I tell mine

Both of us discharging the shit
Of our lives in a world gone mad with itself
Spilling our laughter and pain
Freed from time
We find ourselves
Delivered to the dawn
Delicate, fragile
No longer alone,
No longer denied
A solitude shared
Where men might cry

When I take my leave of you
I will carry your features
Your soft eyes
Affixed to mine
Your naked smile
Your innocence borne
My breath in halt
Wordless
Silent
Discovery
Blessed

I will carry your city
Your people, their essence
Fixed on the map of my memory
I will carry your thoughts
In conversations on the bus
I will carry your smile
As a work of fine art

My new found self
One with you
We shall both
Be changed
For the rest of time

And from our graves to meet
We shall rise to the call of battle
We shall rush on the waters
Fly on the winds
Arrive at the scene of blood fire
Angels of deliverance

Summon our descendants
Offspring and kin
To cast out their fear
Pick up the torch
The light is the way
The way we had trod
To the crossroad of
Fulfillment
Complete
Calling
All the children
Home

Moe Seager

When Ibrahim Fell

The moment comes
Inevitable rendevous
Fusing space and time
Life and death, join face
Shadow flesh
Ghost freed from the bone

You cease to think
Now, you truly feel
Nerves detach, blood racing
Limbs, joints, even the head, useless
Only the eyes and ears, open
Open as never before

When Ibrahim fell
While tending the olive grove
The pain was quick
The end to years of tender toil
His struggle to love to struggle to live to
struggle to be
Ceased in a flash, a silent stream of blood
At the base of his beloved olive tree

Assassin came forward
A small kill, you gloat
A frail man made corpse
Supine so in silence
A severed root
Fruit for the flies
Returned to the earth
Birds flee the trees
Screech shrill and shock

Oh life can be cruel
As you sense failure
A haunting defeat
Overcome in this presence
Your victim's composure
A smile on his face
A moment all his
You will never know.

Moe Seager

The Wind in the Morning

The man wakes from dream
to nightmare,
his night-aged knees
buckling
over rubble
outside when he emerges
from the black mouth of his house

its burnt shell a meager shelter
from the wind
now tugging at a loose something
and the blight it brings
like a scythe through the valleys.

Let the sun rise if it must.
Let it burn through the wind.
Let it dry them eventual white
and broken as the earth—
his neighbours the two lovers

charred in copulation
on the blackened bed
as if they unleashed the starbursts
of the bombs,
that burning burning out their love.

What's left are the wind-worn harvests:
the neighbours' ache,
friends' unanswered calls,
a mother who cries,
who wanders
until death
among the millions of the unconsoled.

We who also wake
but turn away cowed, unshamed,
we whisper only to each other
of the murdered and the maimed:
single, multiple, mass—
the killing fields the index of our regress
back from Auschwitz-Birkenau.

Rustum Kozain

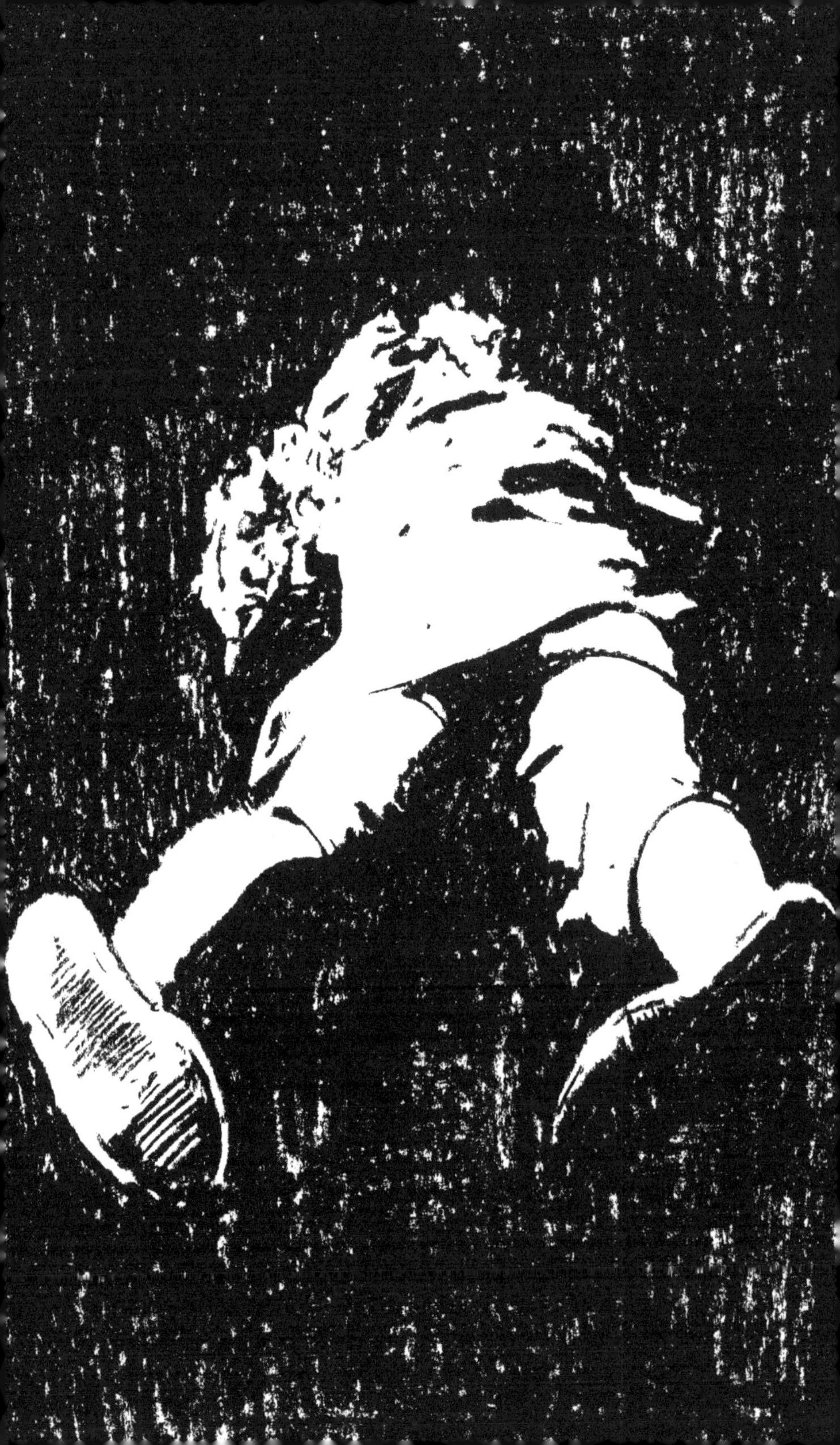

Cours, pour jouer avec tes amis.
Cours, pour te jouer de tes ennemis.
Cours, pour arriver premier.
Cours, pour mourir le dernier.
Cours, pour attraper la balle.
Cours, pour éviter les balles.
Cours laver tes vêtements de cette poussière.
Cours laver tes vêtements du sang de ta mère.
Cours jouer à cache-cache avec tes copains.
Cours trouver ta soeur déchiquetée sous des parpaings.
Cours écouter ton père te lire une histoire.
Cours regarder les grands oublier la leur.
Cours et choisis de rester un enfant.
Cours pour ne pas mourir un enfant.

Cours.

Michel Jovet

स्वगोज़ा

मैं भूखा हूँ यह सच है, तुम भी भूखे हो यह सच है|
मुझे जीने की प्यास मार रही, तुम्हें जीतने की यह सच है|
गुनाहों से न मिटती है सत्ता की भूख, क्या यह तुमको ज्ञात नहीं?
काया को मेरी तुम निचोड़ रहे हो, क्या यह सच्ची बात नहीं?

अस्त्र तुम्हारे प्राणों से बड़े, जो मार दिए कितने बच्चे-बूढ़े,
करने जयजयकार अब तुम्हारी, देखो कितने हैं शरीर पड़े!
कहीं खून की बाढें, तो गिरी बारूद की बरसातें कहीं!
ग़म किसी मौत का तुम्हें भी था, क्या यह सच्ची बात नहीं?

क्या अंतर तुम में-मुझ में, और ख़ुदा में तुम्हारे-मेरे?
डर रूह पे दीमक है बना, आतंक ने घरों में बनाये हैं बसेरे!
सीमाएँ देशों की बदल के, स्वर्ग तुम जाओगे सही...
पर मिलोगे उन्ही बेकसूरों को वहाँ... क्या यह सच्ची बात नहीं??

झाँको अपनी रूह के अंदर... बोलो, यह सच्ची बात नहीं?

The title 'Swargaza' is a word invented by the poet herself. In Hindi/Sanskrit it could mean 'swa'—the prefix 'self' as in 'Gaza herself', or 'swar'—Sanskrit and Hindi for voice-tone, as in 'the voice-tone of Gaza' or 'swarg', 'heaven', as in 'the heaven, Gaza'.

Swargaza

It's true that I am starving; and so are you,
I'm dying of my thirst for living;
while you, of Winning—a truth I tell you!
Crime can never satiate the greed for power—
you're aware, aren't you?
Ruthlessly squeezing my soul you are, is this not true?

O your weapons so powerful,
have killed the young and the old,
And to sing your glories now, the corpses lie, behold!
Floods of blood and showers of bombs,
are all that are in our view,
A life lost, or two, did move you too,
is this not true?

What makes you and I different?
And our Gods from each other's!
Terror sojourns in our homes
and leeching on our souls is Fear!
For sure you will adorn the heavens,
the man that defined boundaries anew,
But you shall have to face there,
the innocents you killed—is this not true?

Peek inside your soul once again and ponder—
Is this not true?

Dr Radha Valaulikar

I am Not in Gaza

A friend gave me this house on the Olympic peninsular in which I sit and write this, a friend who is a poet and a writer. I met her a long time ago, in the time before my mother died, before I was diagnosed with cancer, before my first book came out, before my oldest daughter lost herself and before I spent years trying to understand exactly how, before a middle daughter wrote of her mother as being like a bottle of perfume left with its cap off in an open field, before my youngest daughter broke first one ankle, then another, before marriage became something to eviscerate not live.

I met her when I saw her lying on a couch among the many other writers who were walking around, drinks in hand, conversing in diffident animation the way writers do. It was my job to serve those drinks, and circulate. I saw her and I went over to her, knelt down and embraced her. I yield to the things that possess me, however ill-advised or out of the norm. And this poet, this woman, let me. She let me and we talked about illness and loss. The loss of friends.

Six years later she gave me this house in which I sit with my three daughters, a last time together before the oldest leaves home. A last time of many things. We have sat together and looked out each day over the changing colors of the Pacific, today cresting in white tops, the mountains beyond, the American dream of last resort, O Canada. We have climbed mountains and immersed ourselves in clear lakes created by glaciers. We let Mt. Rainier look back at us and then stepped off narrow ditch-lined roads to brave surging waters off the designated safe routes. We created spectacles of ourselves running for ferries, barely made. We guarded our safe-time, this other-time, bliss-time with determined unity.

And then, when the news came, we drove past the lilac festival in Sequim to do what needed to be done.

Free Free Palestine!
Occupation Is Justified When People Are Occupied!
Free Free Palestine!
Stop Killing Mothers Now!
Free Free Palestine!
While You're Shopping Bombs Are Dropping!
Free Free Palestine!
Stop Killing Children Now!
Free Free Palestine!
From The River To The Sea Palestine Will Be Free!
Free Free Palestine!

My daughters have grown up in a house where Palestine is real. That house is set in a neighborhood of Orthodox Jewish people who do not speak to us. They attend public schools where Jewish holidays are observed. They go to the bat mizvahs and bar mitzvahs of their friends. They sit through Hebrew services in honor of those friends, and dance the nights away, but they do not wear the requisite sweatshirt announcing their participation and, by design, the exclusion of the uninvited, to school the next day. My oldest daughter braved the censure and ostracism of her high school classmates to write about Palestine for her school paper. She did so even when she knew very little about this place. She did so because she wanted to know more and wondered why nobody ever said the word Palestine in her school. She did so and was publicly ridiculed even by her closest friends, but privately commended by the "others" in her school, the Syrian student for instance, writing her a message on Facebook to thank her. The middle daughter, a defiant non-conformist had asked now and again for a BDS shirt that she planned to wear to school. Despite all this, neither of them knew what they were being passionate about.

Until they marched. Until Free Free Palestine! became their chant, became the uncomfortable thing to shout, these girls who had never shouted anything before, before they were willing to stand in silence, red-tape across their lips to signify the silencing, before a large and joyous rally of supporters of Israel, the Magen David in its bright blue against the white, the slogans and placards denouncing the usual. Every now and again they would lift their own placards to cover their faces and ask me questions. About Hamas, about human shields, about tunnels, about the precise dimensions of Palestine, about history, so vast, so vast, so reducible at times like that.

To this: Imagine a prison
To this: Imagine yourself unable to move from this square to that rooftop
To this: Imagine roads you cannot cross
To this: Imagine your eleven year old sister dying in the streets
To this: Imagine you have nowhere to go, nowhere to hide, and that nobody cares.
To this: What would you do?

They were willing to forego things they had intended to do in order to join these people they had never met before. In order to hold the banners bigger than themselves, to face down a police barricade, to say yes, with enthusiasm, when asked if they wanted to march again, to try to figure out where the president, rumored to visit, was going to be so they could lift their voices to him too.

For the first time in my life, I was an observer. I wasn't the one decrying the injustice to them, I wasn't the one delivering my speeches about American complicity. For the first time we were equals, equally committed. They, at eighteen and thirteen and eleven, reading the news late into the night, watching videos ranging from the bombing of a beach in Gaza to America's foreign aid to Israel's military, about the beginnings of Hamas. For the first time my eighteen year old daughter was looking at the visual provided by the UK *Guardian* of the 132 children killed by Israel in this latest assault, twelve of those the ages of her younger sisters. For the first time they, too, did not care anymore that their friends would unfriend them, that they would lose followers on twitter and instagram and all the other fora in which popularity is measured. They were willing to let it go. They were willing to say this word, *Palestine*, out loud. They were willing to use the red, black, white, and green as their profile picture. Because they understood at last how that flag was also theirs.

I am not in Gaza. I look out at the blue of waters untroubled by noise and sorrow, worried only by the winds that fleck it in white. But there is a sea-change in this house and we are, in our hearts, our minds, in Gaza. Take heart, Gaza: you have new voices.

Free Free Palestine!

Ru Freeman

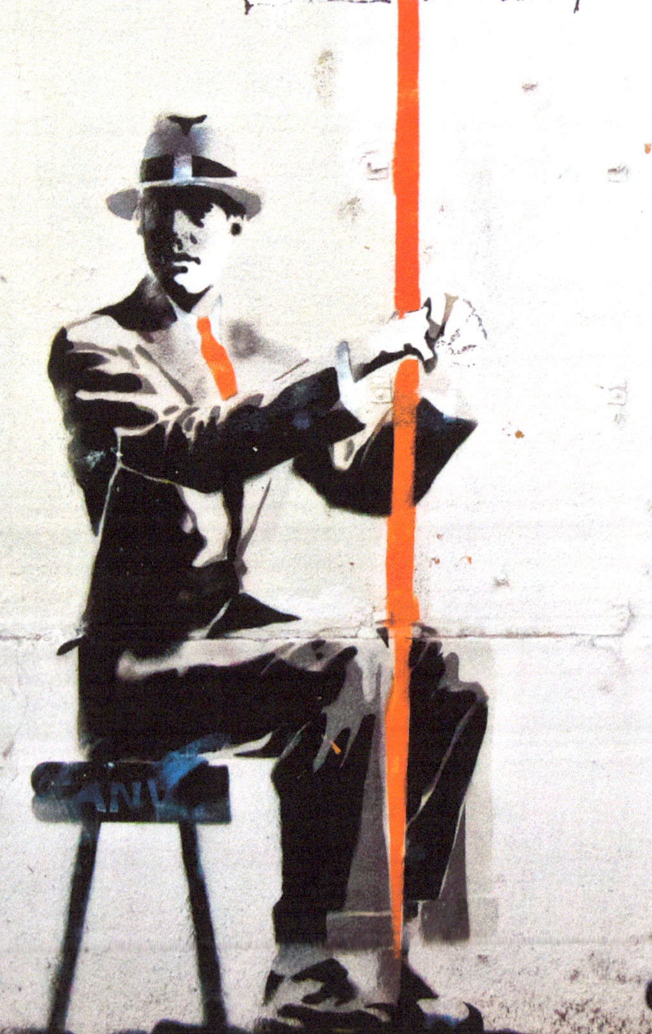
ONCE
WE
WERE
HEROES
CANVAZ

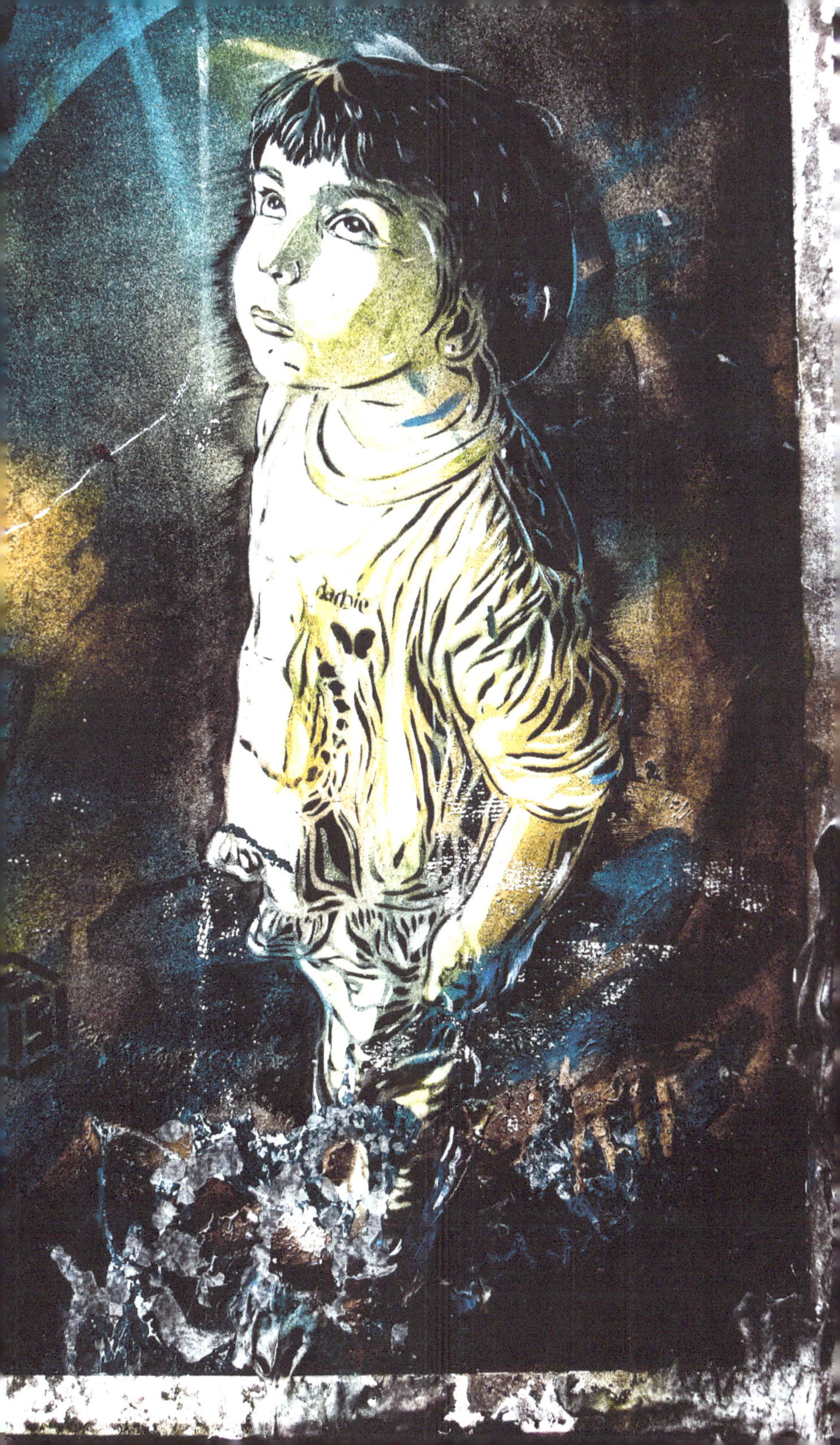

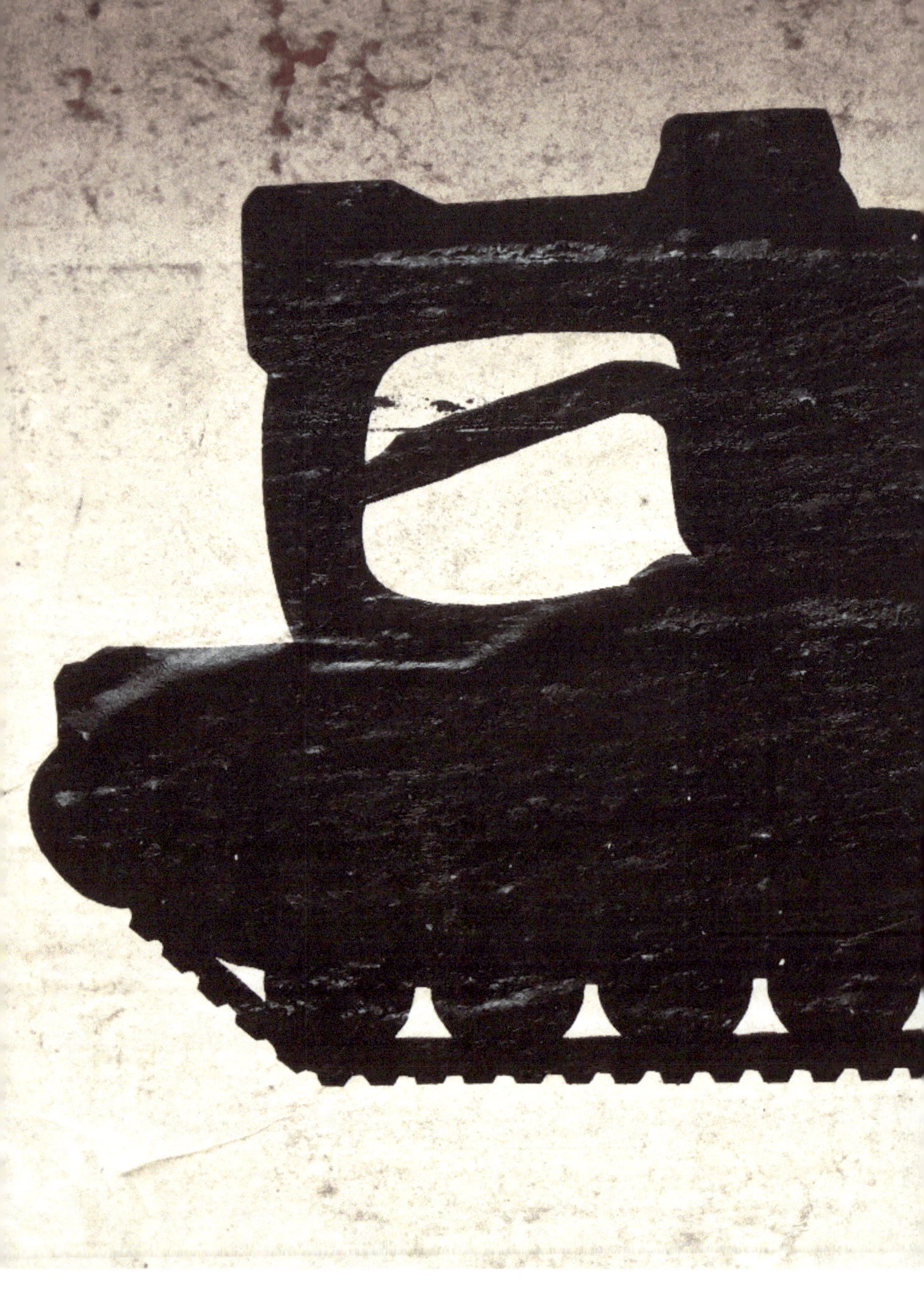

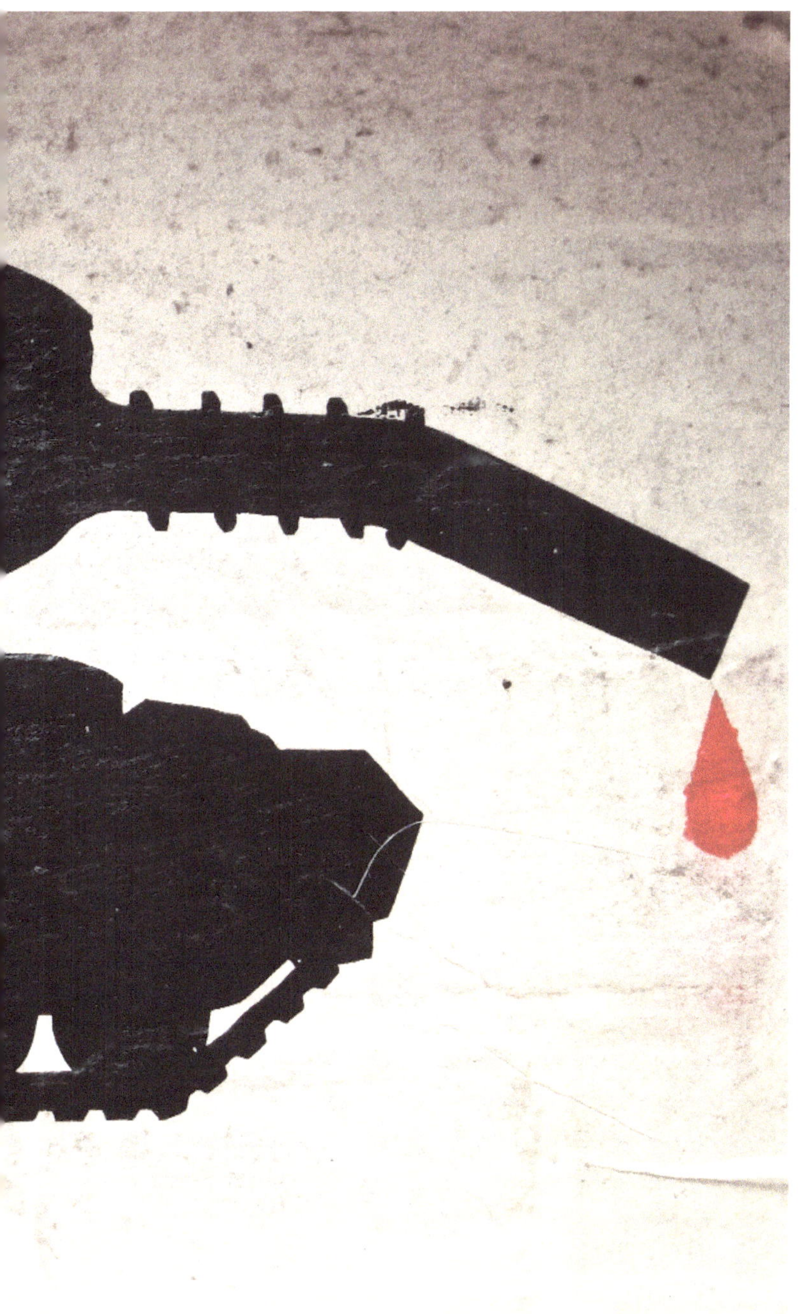

Do You Run?

What do you do
when fireworks and rubble
are made of everyone you once knew?

When you're called to identify your family
by a number of dismembered body parts
and you recognize your mother
by the scarf pin you lent her that morning.

Streets
lined
with shattered souls
and broken homes.

Your neighbor's son sits at the foot of his mother
as he waits for her to wake
and the explosions quake
beneath your feet
until even your tears have lost their heartbeat.

Imagine,

If your friends were in body bags—bloody,
and the only thing more disheartening
than seeing their eyes closed
is knowing that the world will mimic them.

What do you do when you witness brutality?
the rape of your sister?
as they undrape the Hijab from her head,
break through the stitches in her Abaya,
her body quivering still.

When humanity is lost
and the bloodshed turns you into a statistic.

Do you run?
Run like an uncaged lion?
Run with nothing but Allah's name on your tongue,
let them shower you
as bullet
after bullet
plunge through your body
as bullet casing
after bullet casing
fall to the dusty floor,
when your knees buckle
and you meet the earth
for the first few seconds,
do you make eye contact with your dead family
beside you?
Watch the explosions over the horizon
and feel merciful
for the survivors.

Nazlee Arbee

Regime Change

Today we are going to unbomb you,
Today we are going to re-attach your children's limbs,
Knit their arteries back together,
Remake their screams into laughter.
Today we have declared that war can be undone,
Bombs can be recalled,
Shrapnel can be extricated
as if it had never punctured skin and bone,
Memories can be unscarred.
Today we have discovered how
houses can rise in an instant from rubble,
Our miracle-magical builder's kit
can even make home improvements.
Today we have decided that lies can be untold,
News can be unmanaged,
Countries unoppressed,
Fear can be cut quick on the nerve as if it had never
been born. Today the coffins will be vacated,
Body bags will be unstitched,
The undertaker will apply for a job as a florist,
Soldiers will upturn their helmets as plant pots,
Ministers will be made to sign on the dole,
Royals will rise for work washing out bed-pans
And we'll strike a souvenir pendant out of our bullets
for the day when history was unmade.
Today we are going to unbomb you,
Surprise you, surprise ourselves,
We are going to do what no-one has done before,
Wage war on war.

Neil Young

Echoes (I-IV)

'From the river to the sea / Palestine will be free'

My body is in front of you,
In Tuscon.

My head is in Gaza.
That's a privilege,

Of my passport.

The borders of Israel
Stretch far,

As far as the Chihuahuan
Desert—

***

My body is in front of you,
In anger.

My head is in Gaza.
That's a privilege,

Of my resistance.

The borders of Israel
Stretch far,

As far as the Chihuahuan
Desert—

My body is in front of you,
In love.

My head is in Gaza.
That's a privilege,

Of my anger.

The borders of Israel
Stretch far,

As far as the Chihuahuan
Desert—

***

My body is in front of you,
In pieces.

Your head is in pieces.
They are pieces,

Of a wild sustenance.

The borders of Israel
Stretch far,

As far as the Chihuahuan
Desert—

Steve Willey

Oh my people

god had a long song for us
he felt sorry
the world felt sorry
it's soil which curdled and bled
under our feet to say sorry
our blackened soot hands

rivers leaning backwards
birds caught in the tree's limbs
gnashing their beaks
and sighing and loving us
our wings
and soft streaked faces
our book learning

so clever
and sleeves stitched up
against the seam
and those dark eyebrows
and the lamps burning
all through the night
shrouds spun from gold

my people
serrated and burnt
and gaping
always hungry
big liquid eyes
of knowing what happens
always moving and going

and as we were hated we were loved
in our going
our lightness over oceans
crushed apple smells
maths problems
flickered screens
long roads off into the thicket

oh people
stopped
dug into the flat ground
I never bowed my head before
hair in my eye

I know you are angry
I know

I know it

but don't you see that you have let them win
don't you see
the crows migrating
death in the beetle black sand

our shared bloated sea

can't you taste the smoke in your mouth?
you made the smoke
oh my dear people you made it

Rebecca Tamás

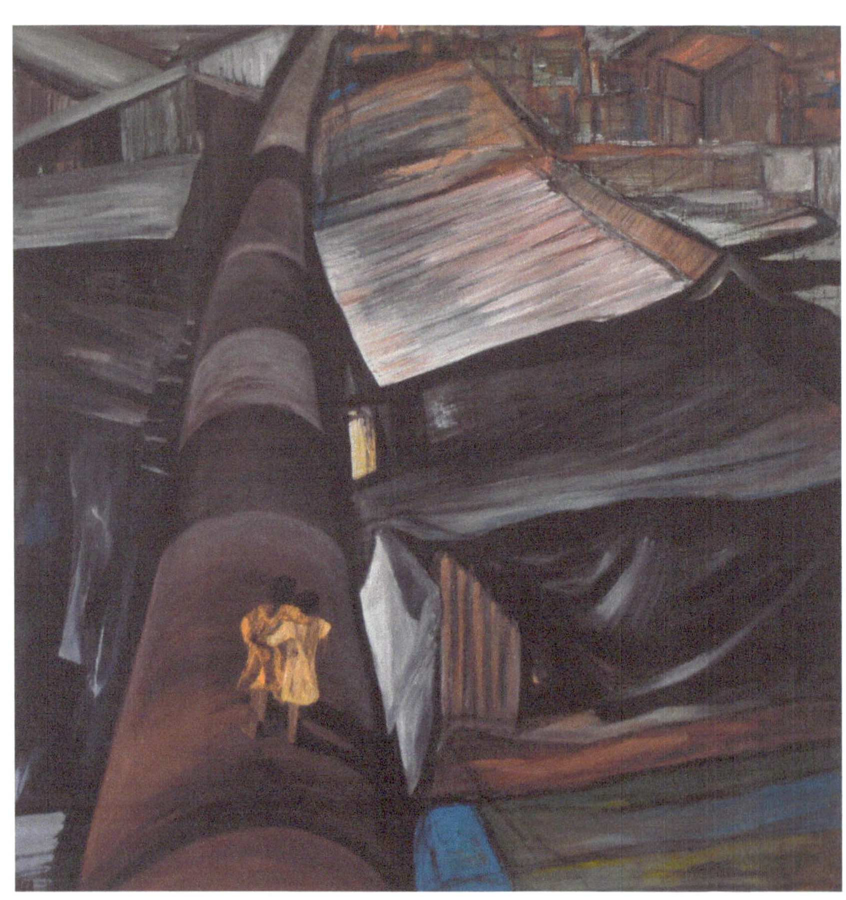

Nuala Herron
The Pipeline
Oil on Canvas

The Sea Lion who Learned to Fly

A female sea lion learned to fly on the night of a storm, when waves were higher than they'd ever been and rocks were strewn with things from the sea, living and dead and somewhere between.

She flew to the cattle field behind the strand and fell to earth by the standing stones where a heifer, at her first attempt, had given up trying to give early birth, lain down and died—but her bull calf had come, after all that.

The next day, when the storm had blown itself out, the cowman came down to check that all was well, and found the new calf asleep against the body of the sea lion—the rich milk on his muzzle smelling strangely of salt, and fish, and sea.

Three Stages of Learning to Fly

Ant

One night in August Ed's wife became an ant. He found her on the pillow in the morning. He smelled the pillow; it smelled of his wife.

"Suze?" he said. Of course, she didn't reply, just waved her antennae as ants do.

It had been a dreadful year for ants. They'd tried everything with varying degrees of success, sprays, boiling water, powder. But now, of course, things had to change. He persuaded her onto a white saucer and chose a bright nail varnish from her dressing table. Then with a single hair from his own head Ed marked his wife with a mote of "New Dawn."

He took her outside to the terrace and put her onto the soil in a large pot containing a slow-growing cactus, one they'd brought back from honeymoon in Acapulco. No matter what they did, there were always ants in that pot.

Now, sometimes, when Ed's reading on the terrace, he finds himself watching these ants. Sometimes he sees his wife.

She is always busy; always going somewhere.

Cricket

Midsummer. The crickets, Ed's wife always said, sounded like telephones ringing endlessly.

"No they don't," he said. "They sound like crickets."

She said he'd see, one day.

Then, that one day arrived and she became a sound in the grass. Perhaps she was a cricket. She'd always been a little person, self-effacing. Ask anyone. They'll all say, "Who?"

Now, her sound rises from the grass and spills out of their garden into the next. Up and out until the whole street, the neighbourhood, then the city is filled with the sound of Ed's wife, ringing.

Ringing. Ringing.

Birds

The flock of birds that was Ed's wife wheels from roof to tree to roof.

He thinks she is starlings. Each part of her now flies. Her fingernails, knucklebones, fingers, hands and wrists—so on and so on—she makes a dense and shifting cloud.

One bird is her heart.

As the flock crazes, mosaics, wheels, this bird is now at her centre, then her boundary. Sometimes it breaks away altogether, flies away from the rest. Ed can see it, a dark arrow against the city sky.

The flock circles, plunges, swallows her heart again, so fast he loses which bird it is. But he knows it is back exactly where it belongs.

Vanessa Gebbie

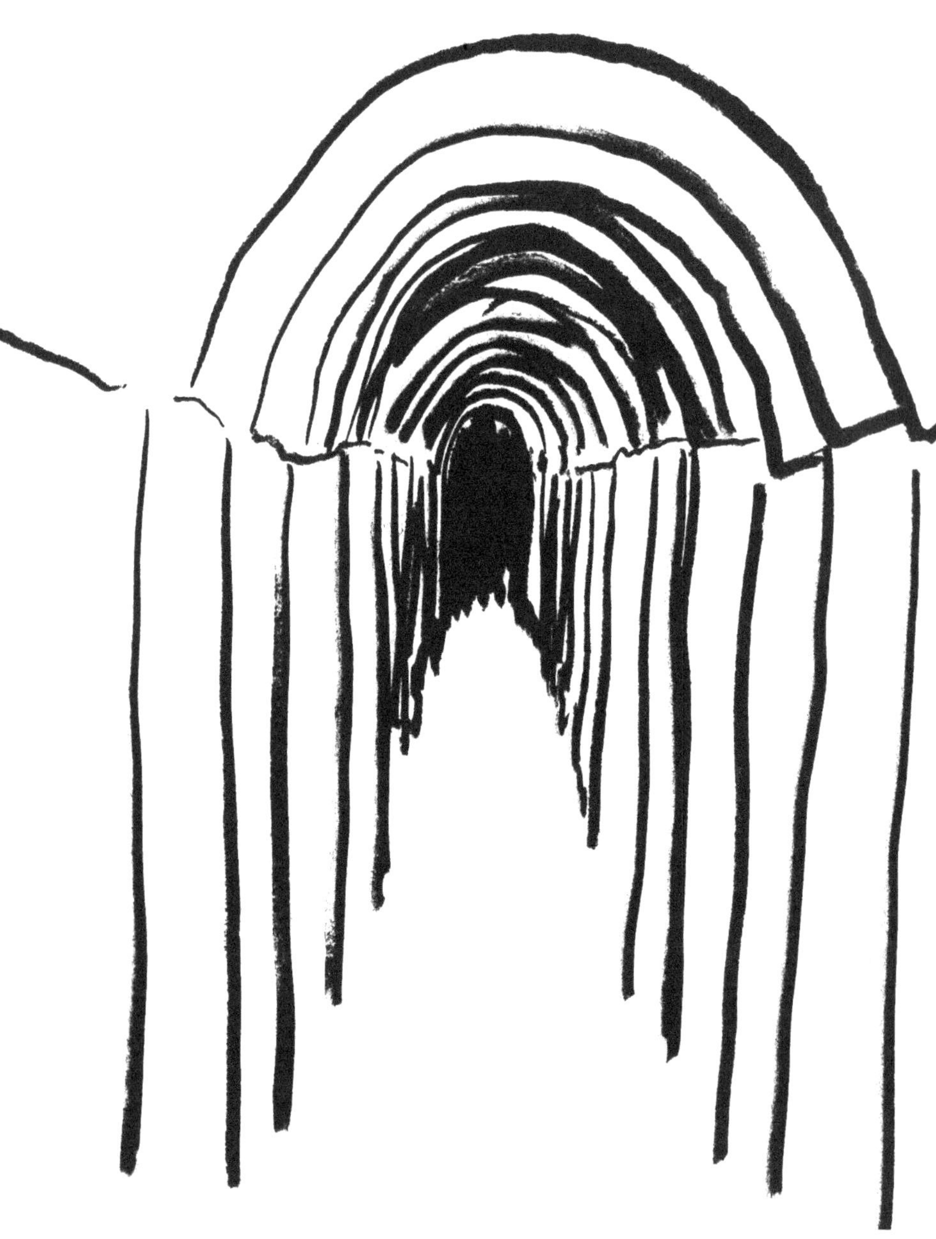

Under Your Skin

Under you we run
The scratch of our spades
The rumble of our discontent.
Burrowing into the foundations
Weakening the surface of your control
Like secrets and threats.
Listen.
Try not to look nervous because the children are watching
Turn up the noise of the bombs.
Amplify the power of your command
Scratch scratch we go.
Under your skin.
As irritating as lice.
Driving fear to distraction
As agitated as fire
You can sense the threat but not see it.
Feeling weaker
Trying to search
Here we are
Behind you
Beneath you.
Gnawing into your spine as you call for help
By the time it arrives, we will be gone.
Into the earth. Back in the safe house.
Knock knock
Here we are again.

Alison Bown

A New Awakening

They said I was different
The enemy
The one to be hated
And wiped out

Peace would be impossible
For you cannot speak with devils
After all

But beyond the barriers
Of prejudice
And beyond the lies
We met

And realized we spoke a single language
Rich with longing for a future free of pain
And we would fight

Children
Raise your voices
Stamp your feet
Shake the world with love

Cristiana Ziraldo

Gaza Hurdy-Gurdy

They shall beat their swords into ploughshares,
their spears into pruning hooks. Isaiah 2:4

The tank slumbers in the heat
a haze of yellow balloons rise from

its grey back, rainbow tracks ease slow
through alleys strung with lanterns

tables laden with fattoush, chorba;
porridge and thyme are for distant,

colder days. The turret-keeper finishes
the carnival song, sends bass notes

down the barrel of his gun, accepts his
stew of meat and okra, his bamia

offered up from the kerb, by a woman
who smiles, begins a song of her own.

Children shriek at the beast,
throw sherbet at its high shield,

music drones from its belly,
an old soldier cranks a hurdy-gurdy,

wheel-fiddles, rubs the strings,
hums the old melody.

Roz Goddard

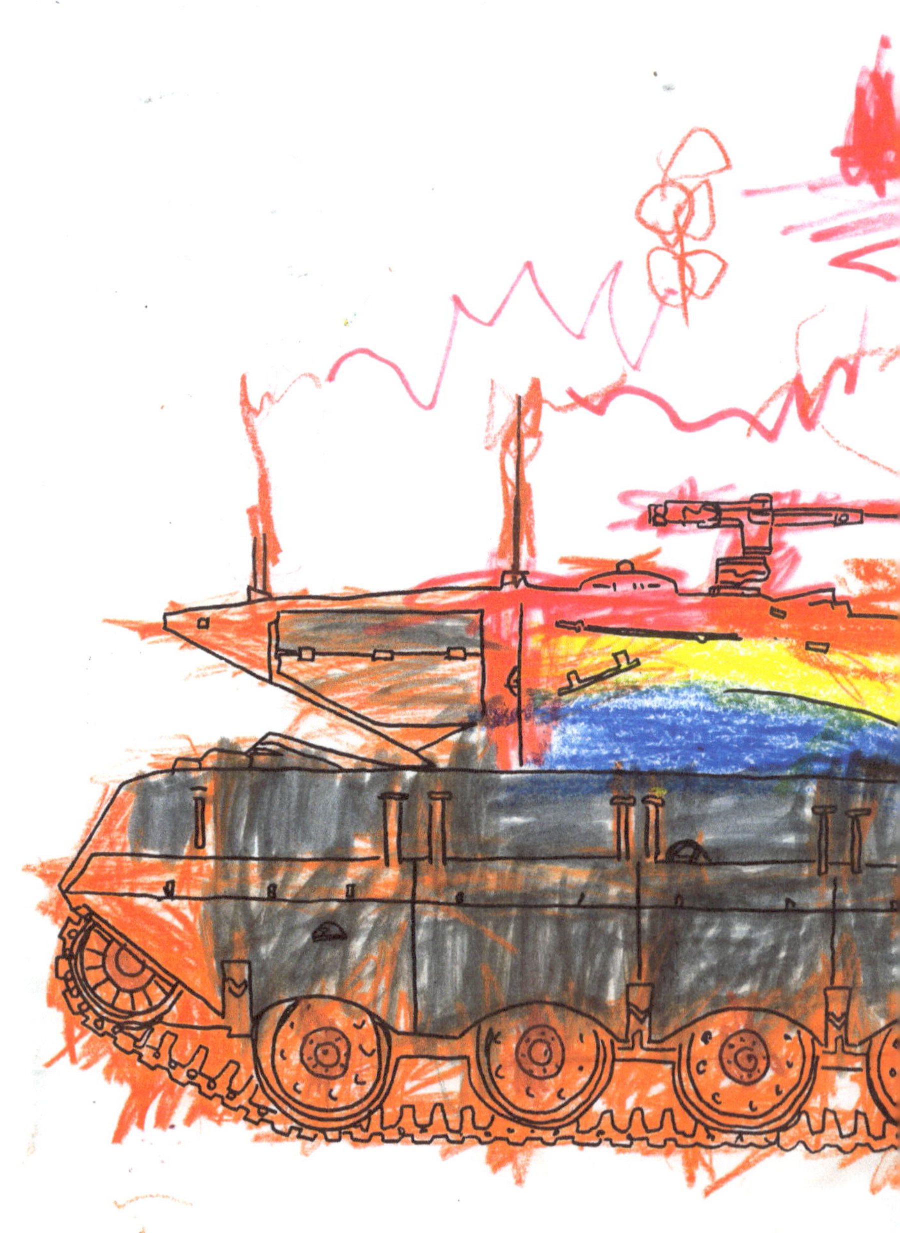

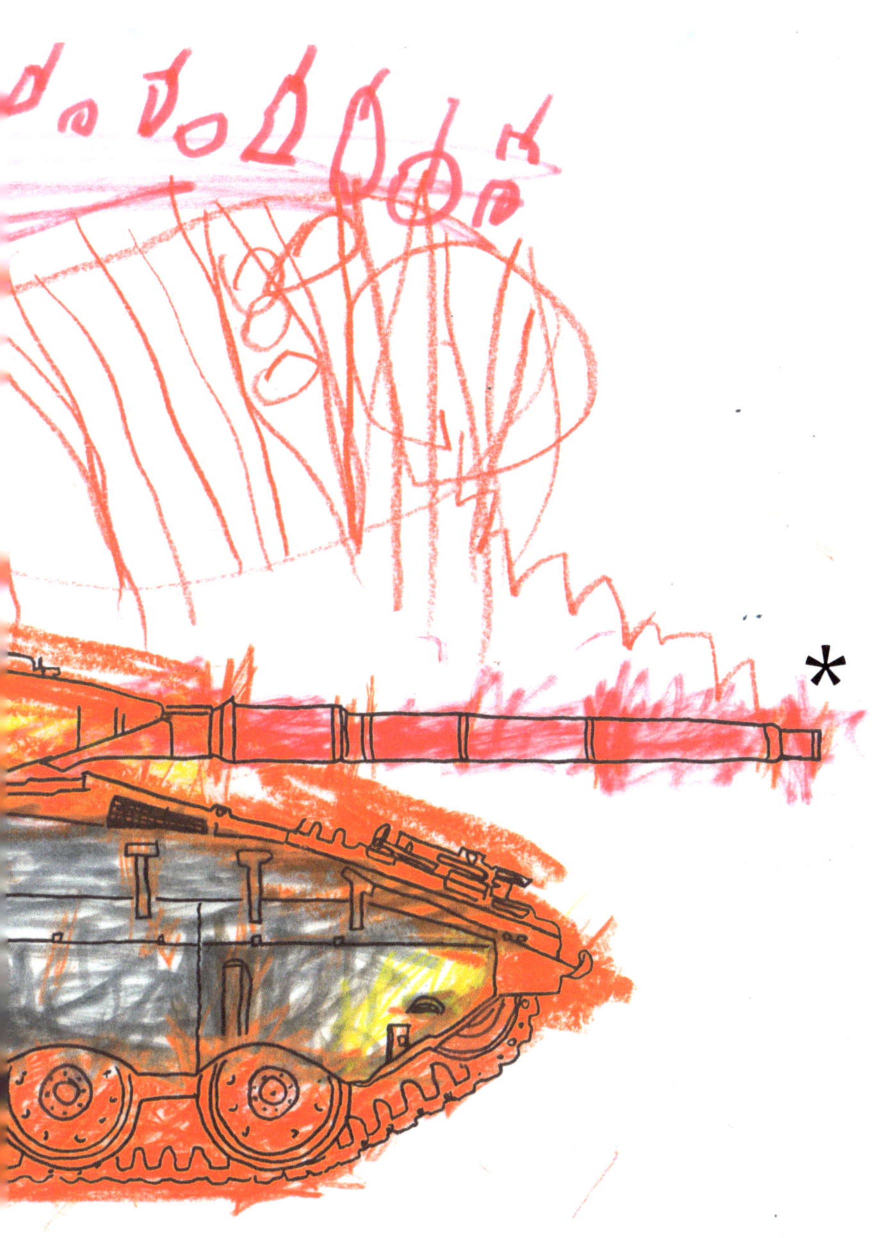

* a tank that shoots flowers and gardens and spaceships
instead of bullets and shells

Pre-emptive Strike

Why wait
        till evil terrorists fire their weapons?
Why wait
        till vengeful men aim their weapons?
Why wait
        till angry teenagers can hold their weapons?
Why wait
        till playful little boys know
        that you're their enemy,
        that you see their will to live, freely
        as their weapons?

We Rise

Ambulance sirens scream
louder, more chaotic shrieks
than normal… (normal?)
like they too have shock and anger
swirling in their shattered hearts.
They fade into weak wailing
cries of mourning mothers,
mothers of the fallen,
all our mothers.

And then empty silence…
that we fill with silent embraces
just to feel closeness,
as if to remind our spirits
that humanity still exists
albeit tainted tonight.

In the cold darkness, love,
love smiles its warmness,
its hopeful light, love,
our gentlest healer,
our greatest need,
our best response.

The fallen will rise,
with love,
we all will rise.

AE Ballakisten

Romain Renault
Flag Drops
Gouache on paper

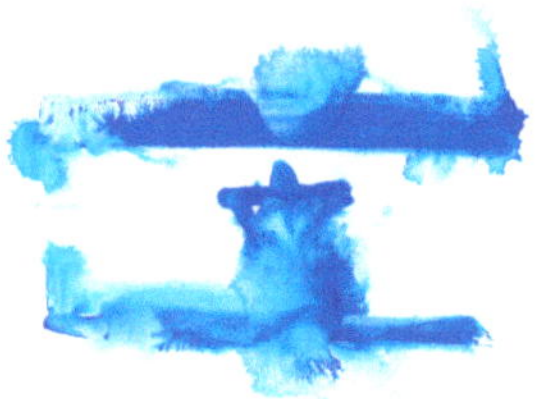

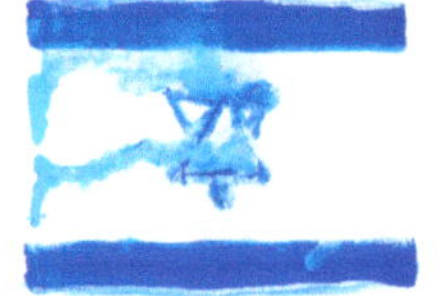

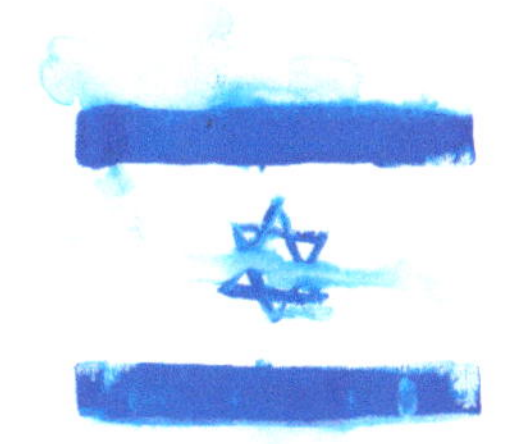

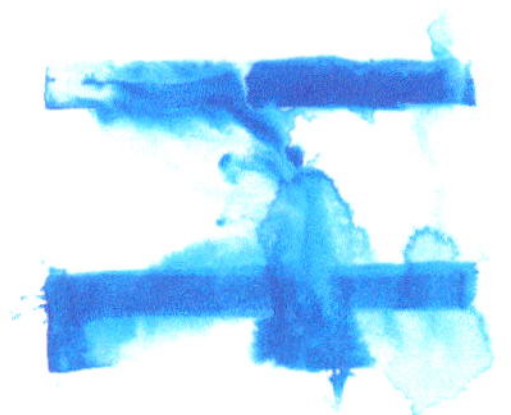

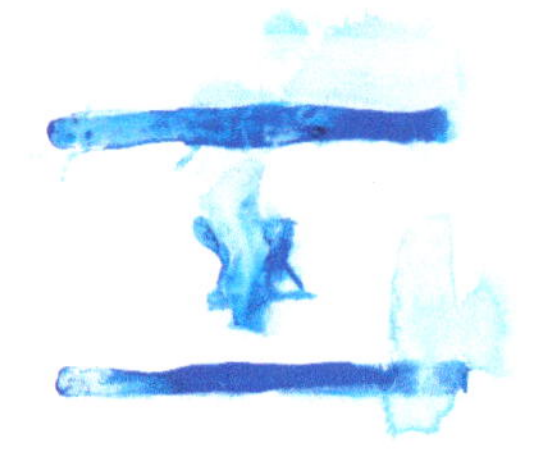

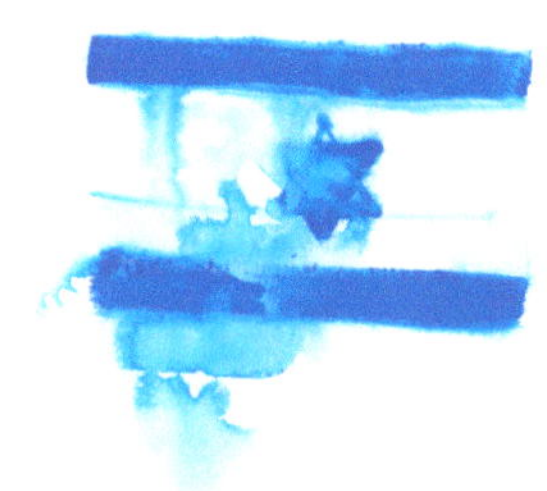

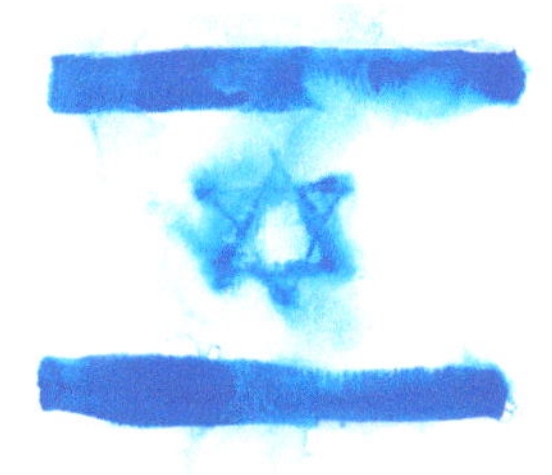

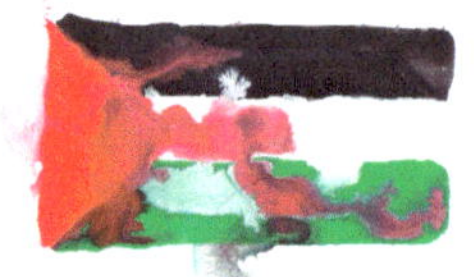

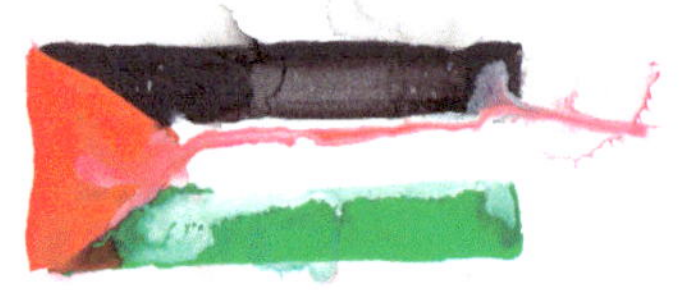

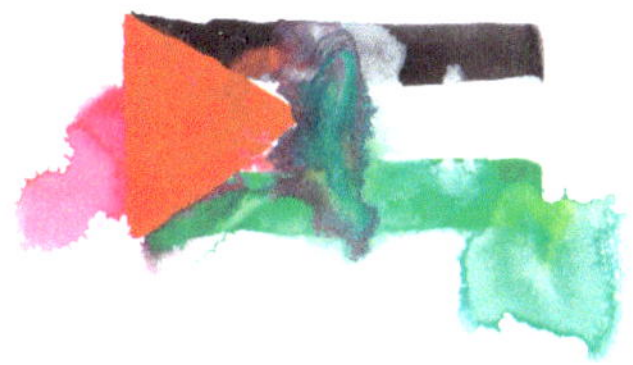

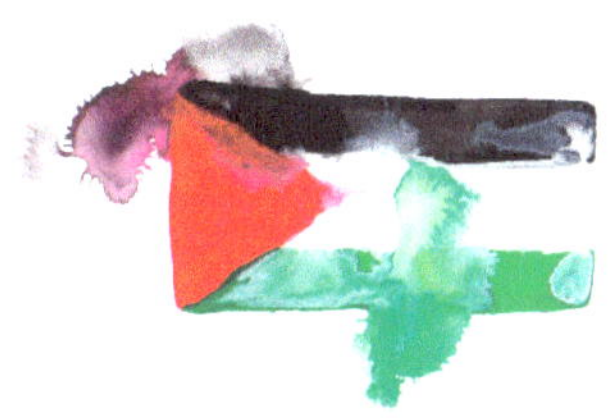

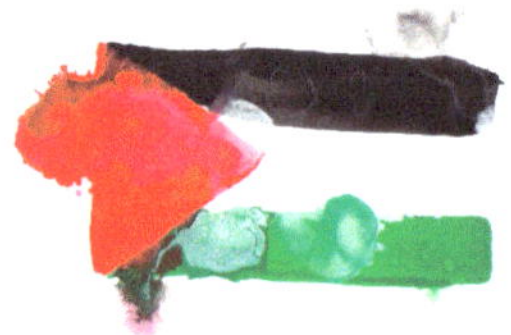

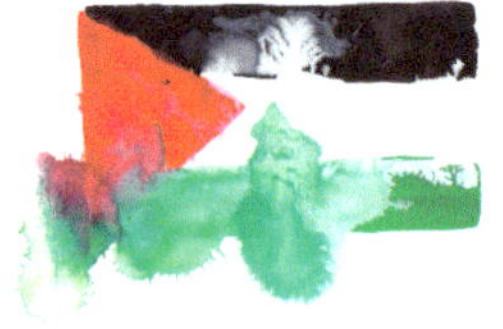

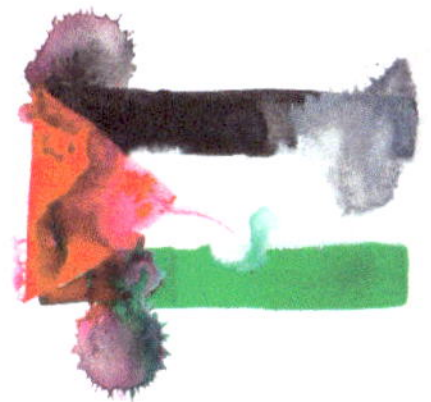

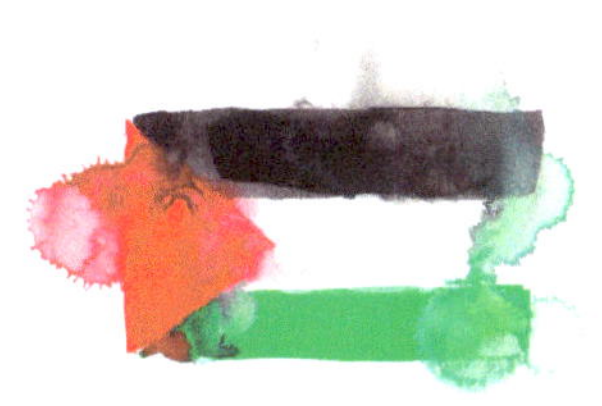

Soraya Hamlaoui
Two drawings
Pencil and collage on paper

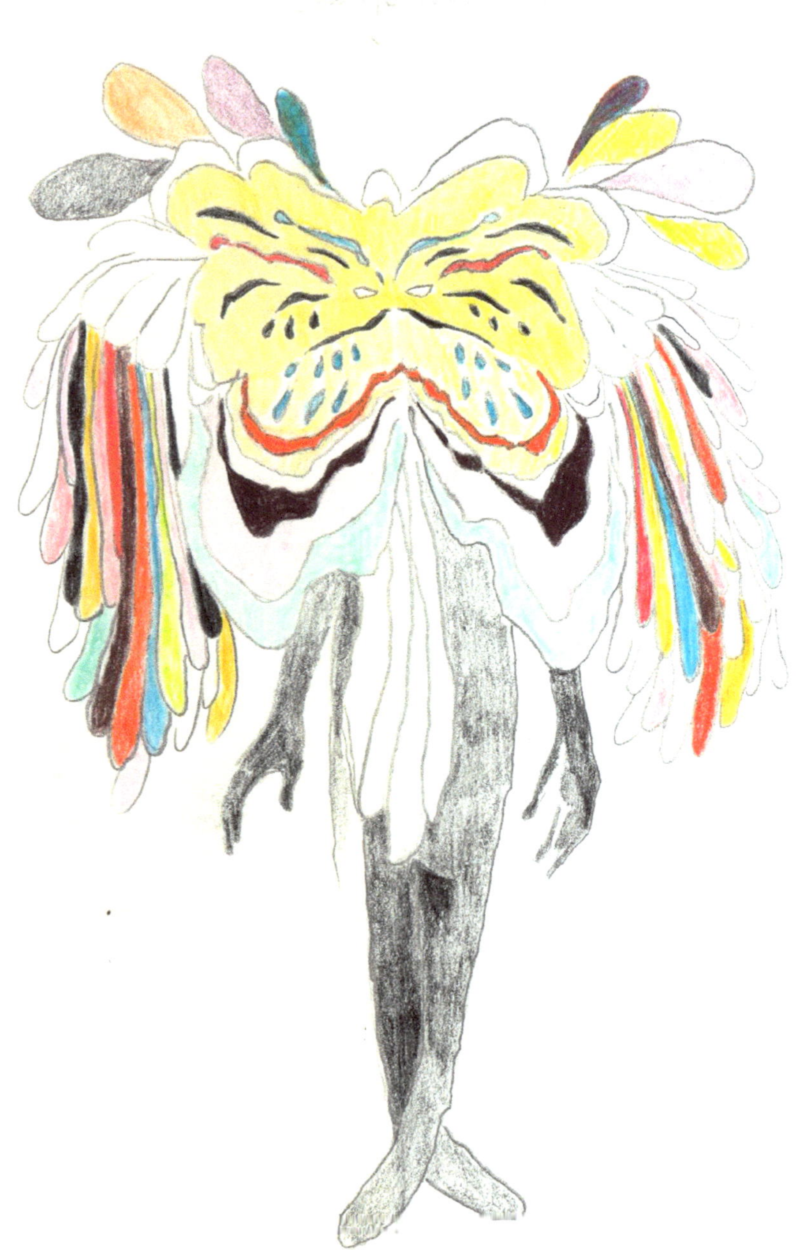

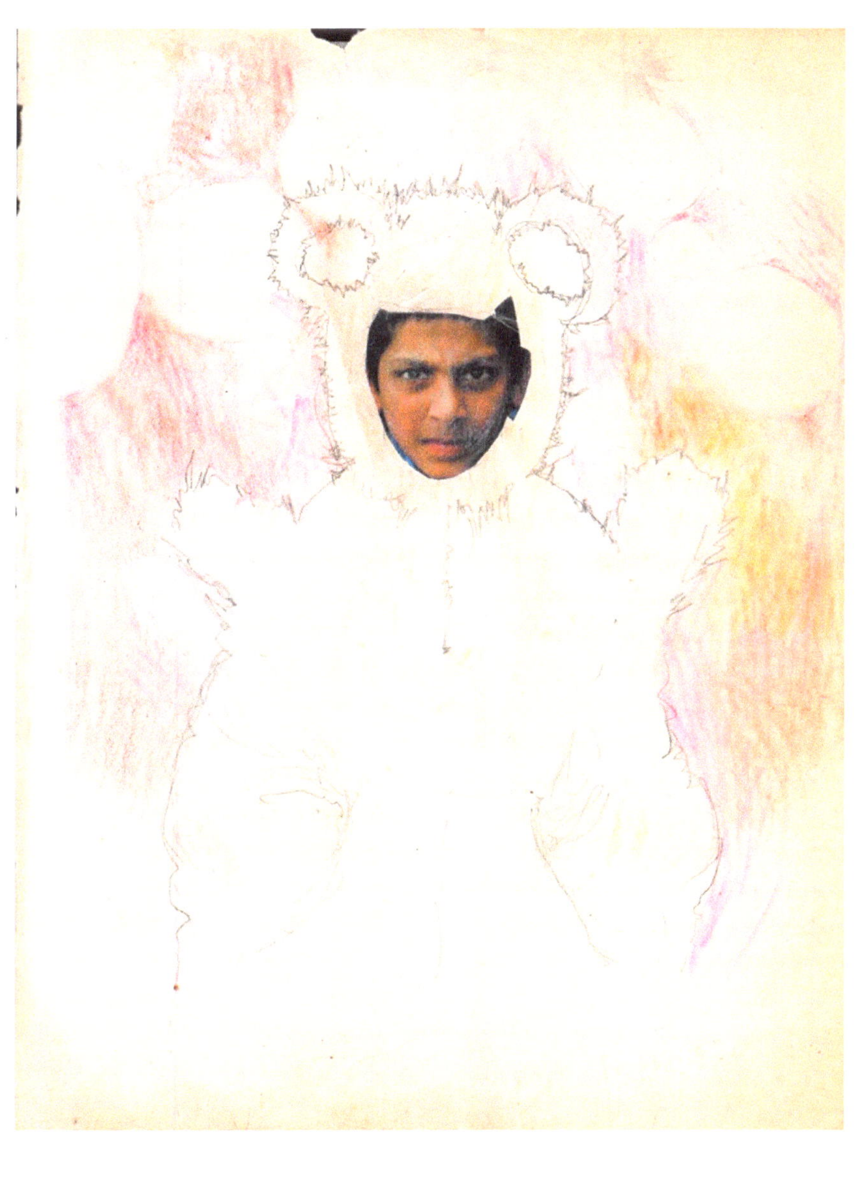

Romain Renault
Nine drawings
Pencil on paper

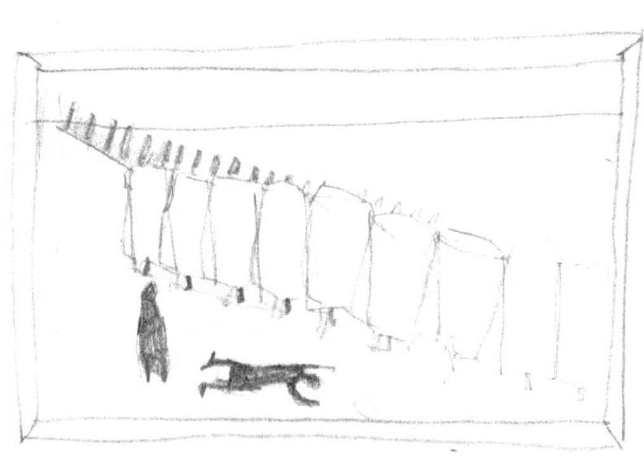

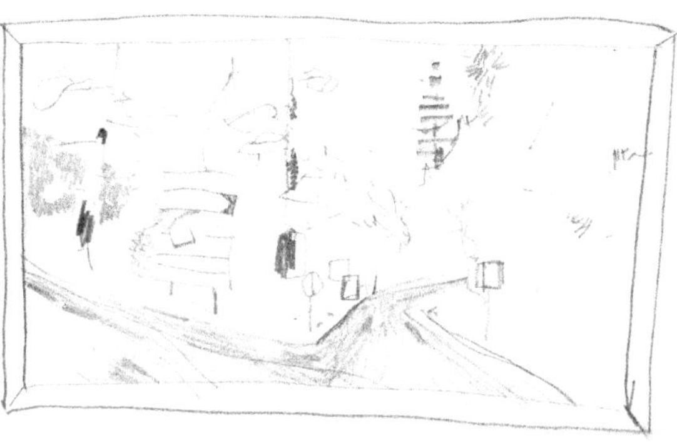

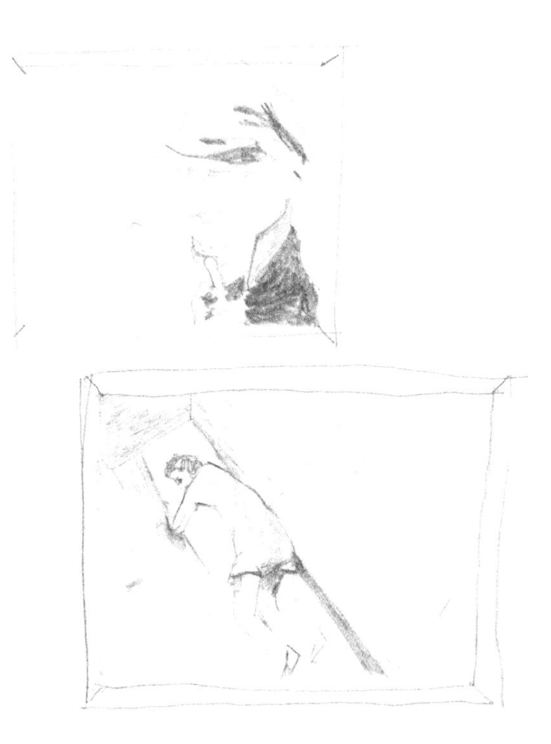

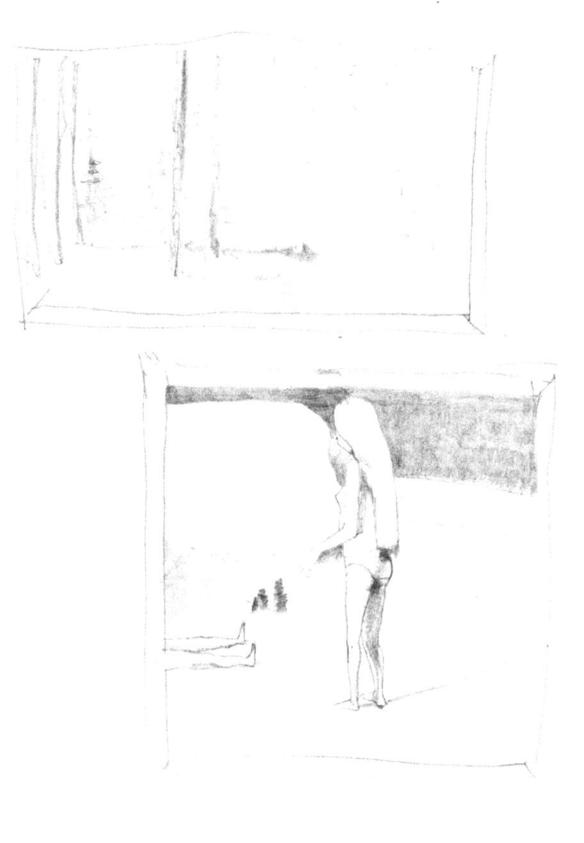

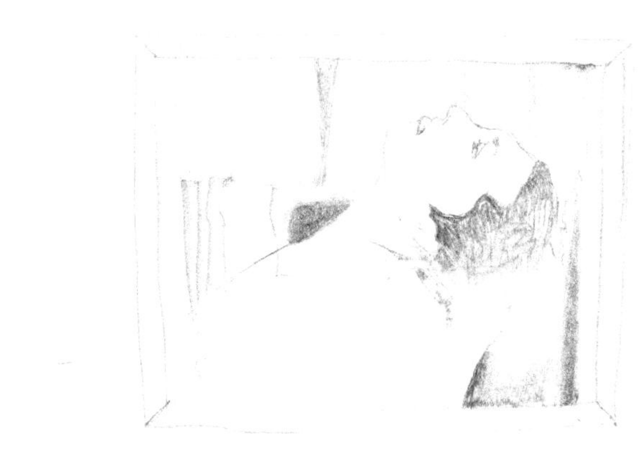

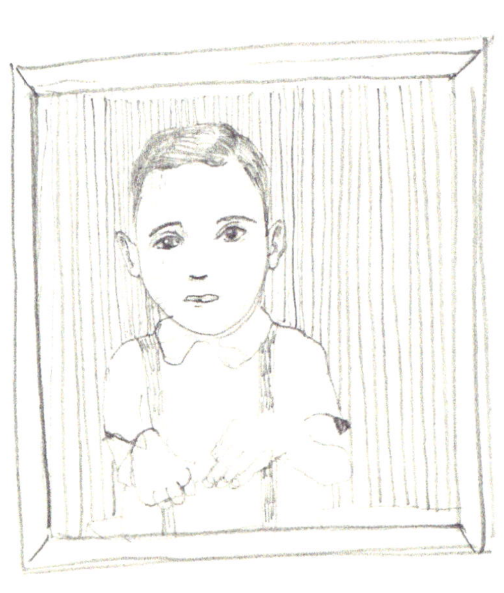

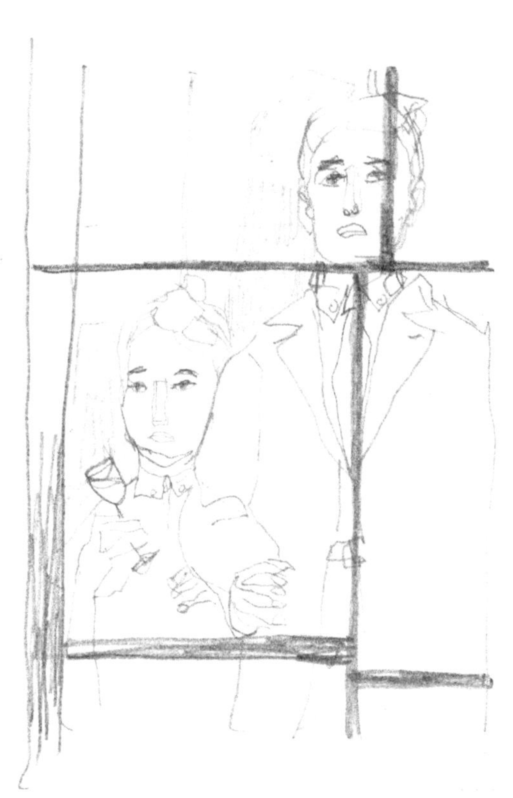

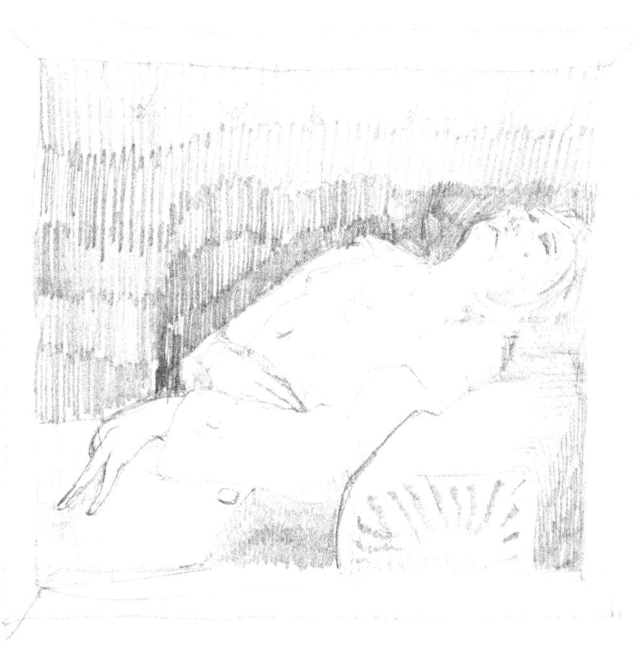

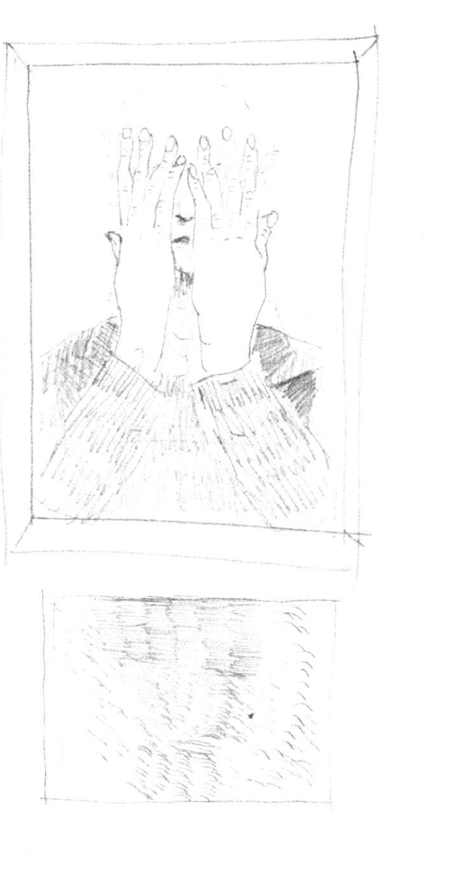

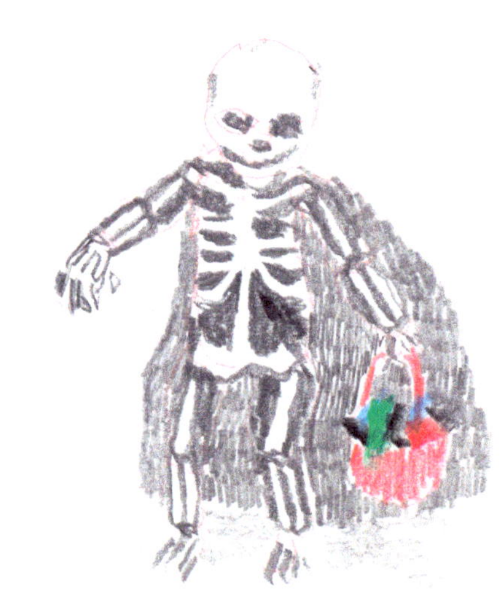

to be born
in a bad place

to be born
in a bad time

to die
before living

before
understanding

is wrong

let us not
hurt too much

let us not
choose to weep

let us not
wound too much

let us not
cut too deep

let us be free
and hide in the
safety of things

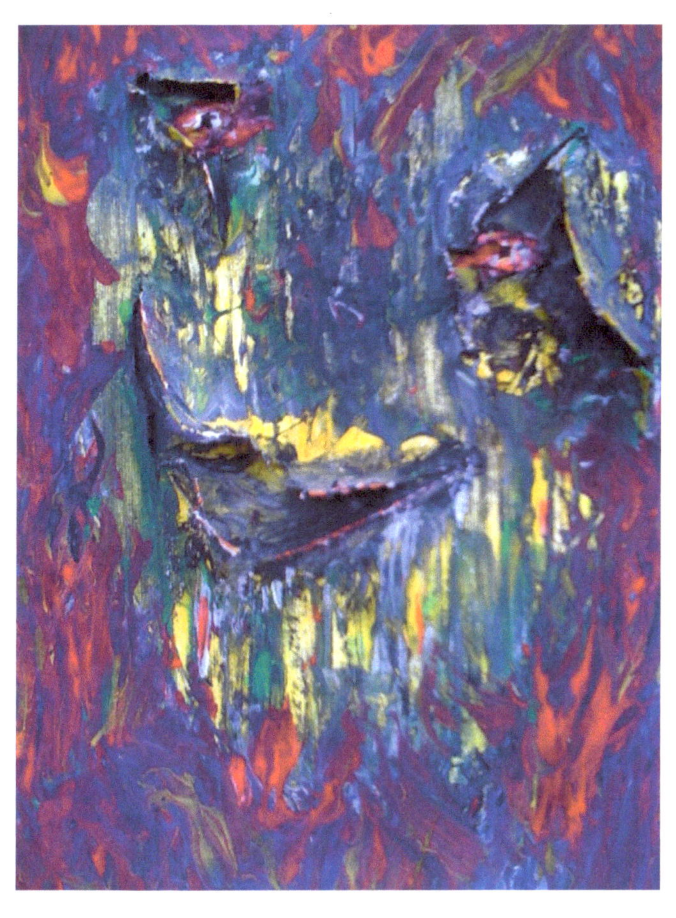

John Staunton

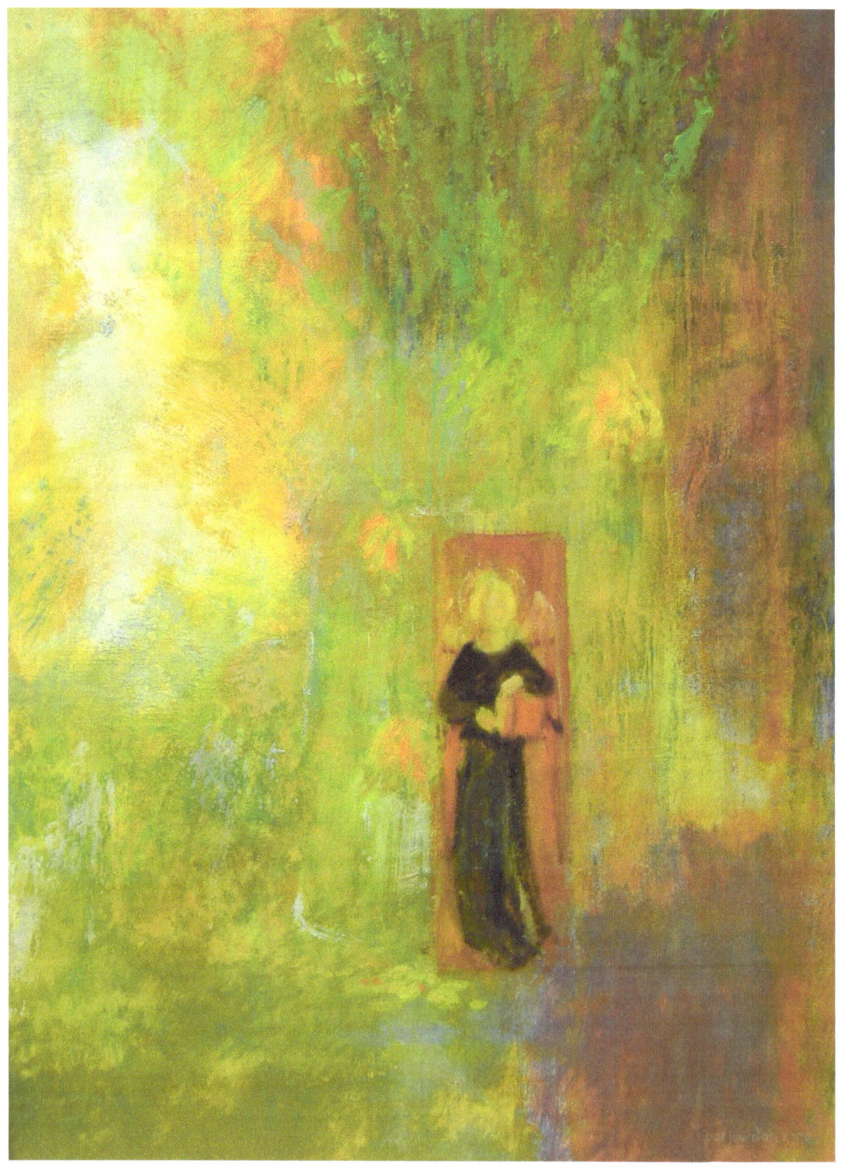

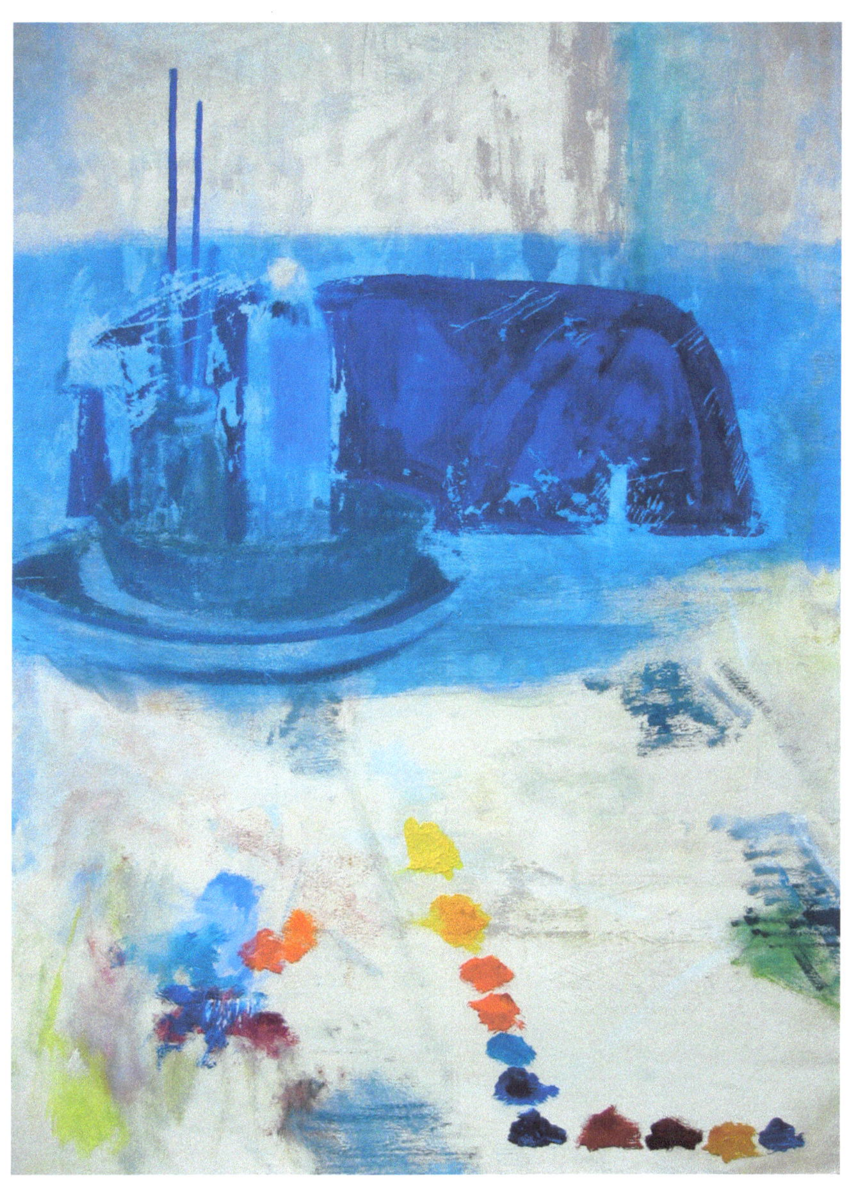

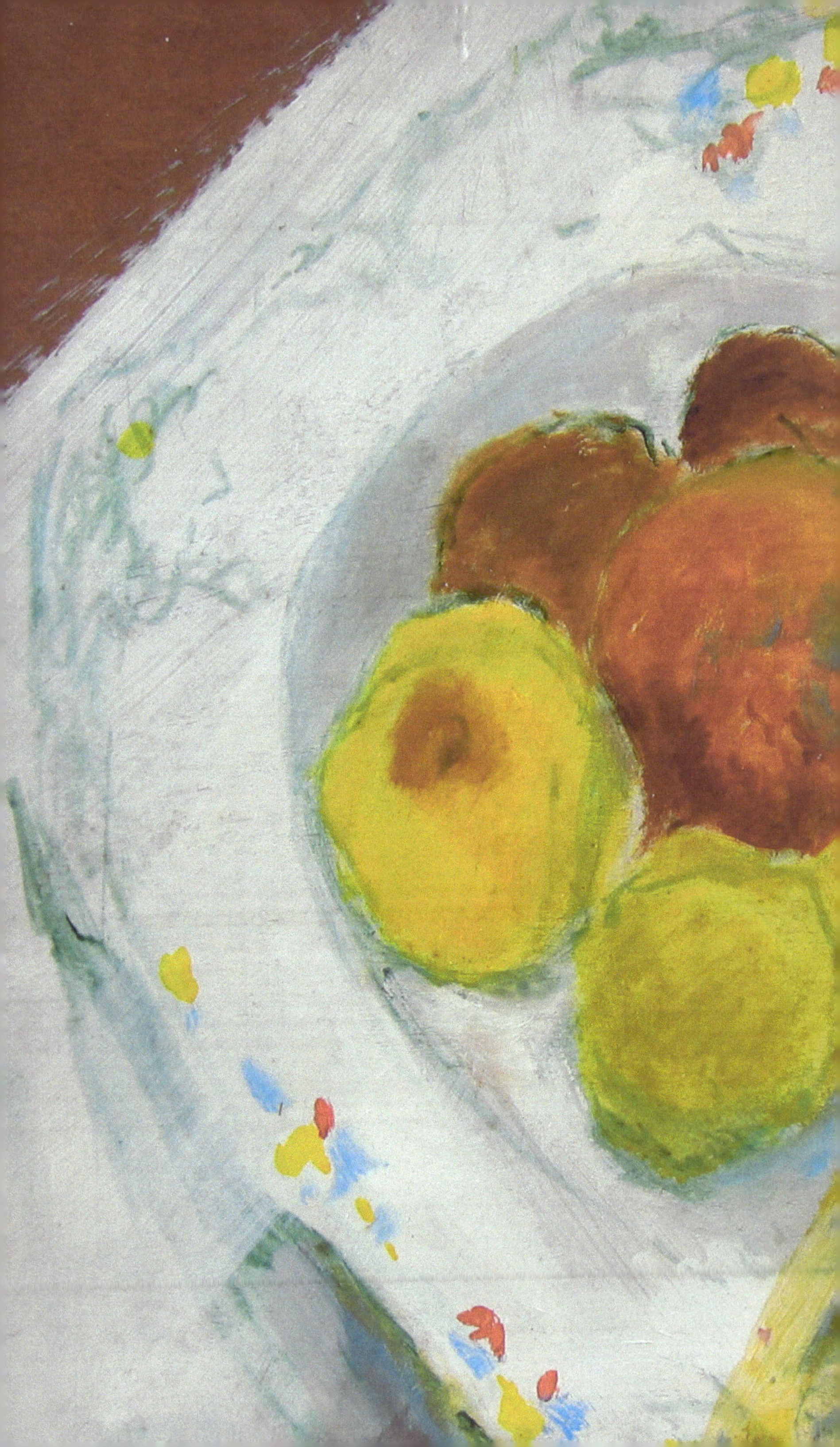

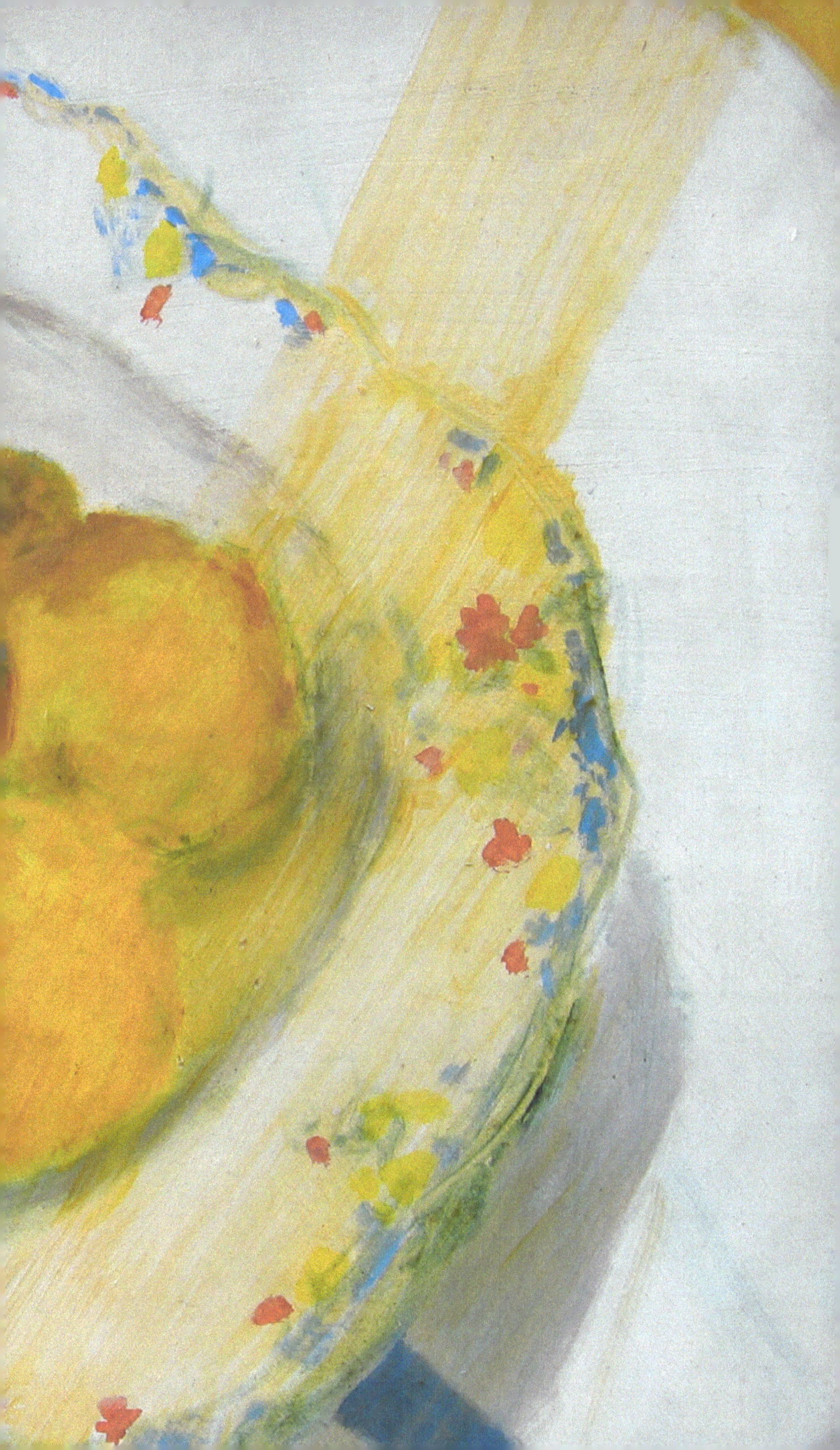

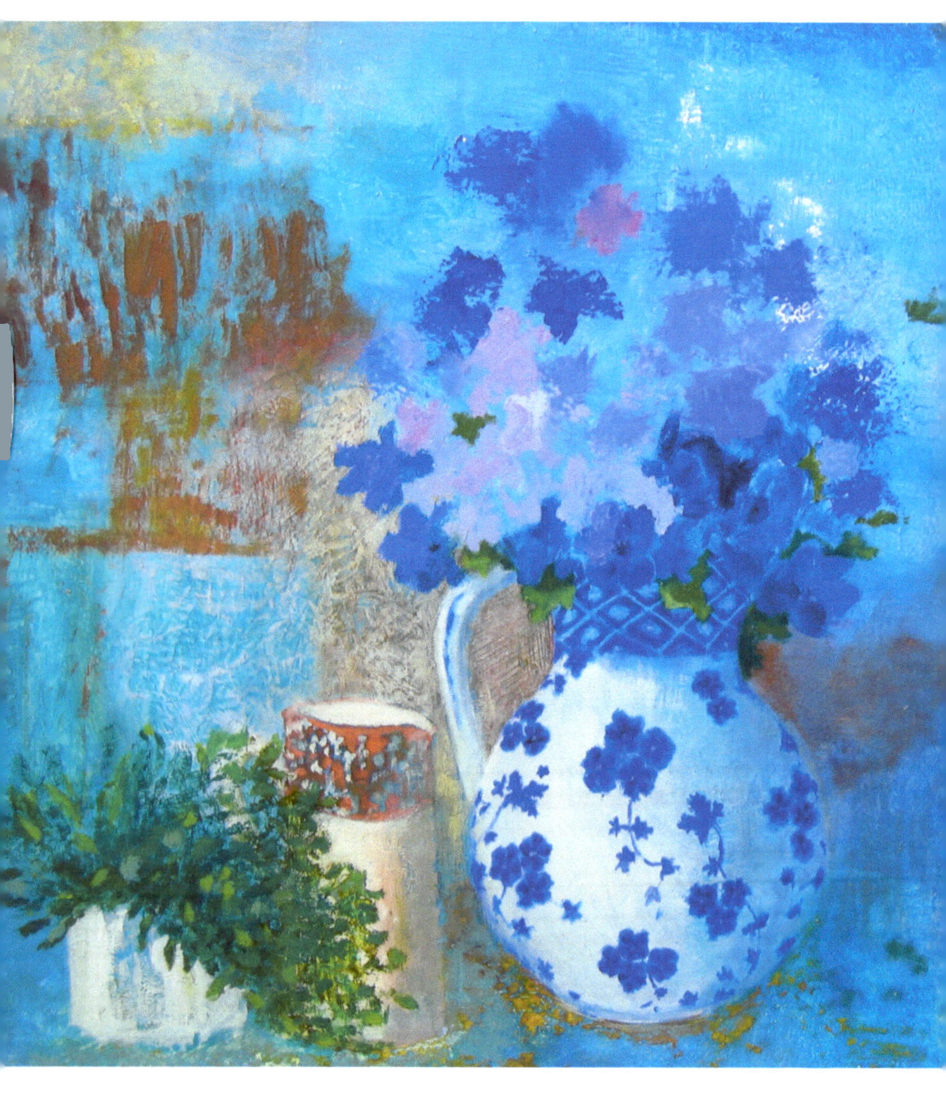

Pat Jourdan
Four paintings
Oil on board

Beyond a Cease Fire: A Letter to Phillip Hammond, British Foreign Secretary

Dear Mr Hammond,

I have just finished reading a short book called *Gaza, j'écris ton nom.* It's a memoir of the days of Operation Cast Lead in 2009 written from the twin perspectives of Christiane Hessel Chabry, Honorary President of EJE, a charity that supports children traumatised by the effects of occupation in Palestine, and Nasser, the operations director for the four EJE centres in Gaza.

It is a timely reminder of what Gazans stand to lose in the current military siege on their land.

UNRWA estimated that 20,000 homes were destroyed in the bombardment in Jan 2009. White and yellow phosphorous were recorded as being dropped in the strip on several occasions. Gas, water and electricity were routinely cut leaving civilians living in putrid homes and streets. Schools were bombed—including many run by the UNRWA as well as those run by Hamas. Hundreds of men, women and children were killed unecessarily as a direct result of the siege. Even those Gazans who remembered the original 1948 *nakba* said that nothing of this level of aggression had been seen before in Palestine. I can only imagine their horror now at seeing it happen for a third time in five years.

I respect your call for a ceasefire and I think that this is the only way to stop the immediate suffering of Gazans and to protect the people of Israel from rocket fire. However I urge you to take stronger action to address the root cause of antagonism: continued Israeli settlement expansion and the ongoing occupation of the West Bank and Gaza Strip. Of course Hamas need to stop firing rockets at Israelis living peacefully in Sderot, Tel Aviv and other cities—this is clear and I appreciate a need to include this in diplomatic rhetoric. But Israeli policy has not moved one inch in nearly 50 years of publicly funded settlement expansion and occupation despite international efforts to the contrary. Did you know that Israel funds illegal settlers with more state money per capita than it does for the Arab citizens of Israel? (*Israel's Palestinians*, Ilan Peleg and Dov Waxman, Cambridge University Press, 2011). The recent peace talks led by John Kerry are understood to have failed dueto the uncompromising position of Mr Netanyahu *vis-à-vis* the settlement programme. By comparison, Hamas has amended its constitution to recognise Israel and the most promising development of recent years (the Palestinian unity government of May 2014) went further to show Palestinian goodwill and adhered to key positions of the EU including the legitimacy of Israel and the renunciation of violence. What compromises has Israel committed to in return?

The 'apartheid wall', as it is commonly termed, is the other great concern for Palestinians, Hamas and international human rights activists the world over. Denounced by a vote of 14-1 in the International Court of Justice and condemned in many UN General Assembly resolutions since its inception in 2002, the apartheid wall concretises the forced incarceration of a country's people. I urge you to press the Israeli ambassador in London on the dubious legality of the wall and the accompanying occupation. Israel has a right to self defence, as do all in the community of nations, but not by 'any means necessary'. One of the ICJ's key findings was that the invocation of security needs does not, in this case, warrant the building of an 8m militarised concrete wall around a densely packed civilian population. Can you give assurances that the UK will live up to its verbal commitment to the Geneva Convention and the EU Convention on Human Rights with action that will ensure human rights abuses will be put to an end by those powers with the means to do so?

There is an urgent need to think beyond the next ceasefire. You have the power to follow your colleague Mr John Kerry's lead and demand that Israel commit to ending settlements and occupation as part of any peace deal agreed, no matter how temporary. I urge you to consider the morality of your position; the authority that you hold demands of you to make decisions in the best interests of the British people and those committed to justice and the rule of international law throughout the world. The time to act is now and I believe that we, the British public, are on your side and the side of direct action.

I ask therefore that you consider sanctions against Israel and a boycott of Israeli goods if they do not commit to ceasing settlement expansion and the ongoing illegal occupation of the West Bank and Gaza Strip. Most pressingly an immediate arms embargo between Britain and Israel should be put in place to send a message that we will not be complicit in crimes committed against humanity.

Only then will the children of Gaza and Israel sleep easily.

Yours sincerely,

Roland Singer-Kingsmith

Consider the Shape of Things

Consider the shape of things:
the round earth, the sun, the moon,
a mother's arms, the cradle of her womb.

Consider a hug, nestling against a heart,
a tiny fist
opening like a desert flower.

Consider childhood, the hope, the teens:
all our tomorrows
planted in their footsteps.

There is no room here
for guns and bombs,
the crazy run of vengeance.

Is it a given we can do no more than wring our hands
and watch TV,
grateful for our children in the back yard?

Consider this:
if we do not stand up for Gaza's children,
who will stand up for ours?

Maggie Harris

Allah is above them

My heart is broken, I can't smile today
I close my eyes... I cry, I pray
But I can't stop, my body shakes harder
Every time I see another sister in Gaza
Every time I see the pain of a father
Desperate to save their children
from becoming martyrs
Have they not seen enough suffering for one lifetime?
Can these children not play without fear, in the sunshine?
Instead they are killed, by snipers, from the air
While the rest of the world ignores, they don't care...
I scream to god, this inhumanity is not fair!
All I see is wilful ignorance, whilst the good despair
Whilst the ignorant continue, with their salaries,
Their calories, a few pennies to charity, this is insanity!
I scream to them: *open your eyes, where is your humanity?*
This is real life, and you are complicit in the tragedy!
Where were you? Why won't you take a stand?
What else could be more important? I don't understand!
Little children killed every day, when will it be enough?
The youngest baby was barely two months!
They are my brothers my sisters from a distance so far
I beg for their protection, *inshallah!*
I retain my hope, because I see peace in the end
In the words of a Palestinean child:
Their jets may be above us
but Allah is above them

Ilhan Tahir

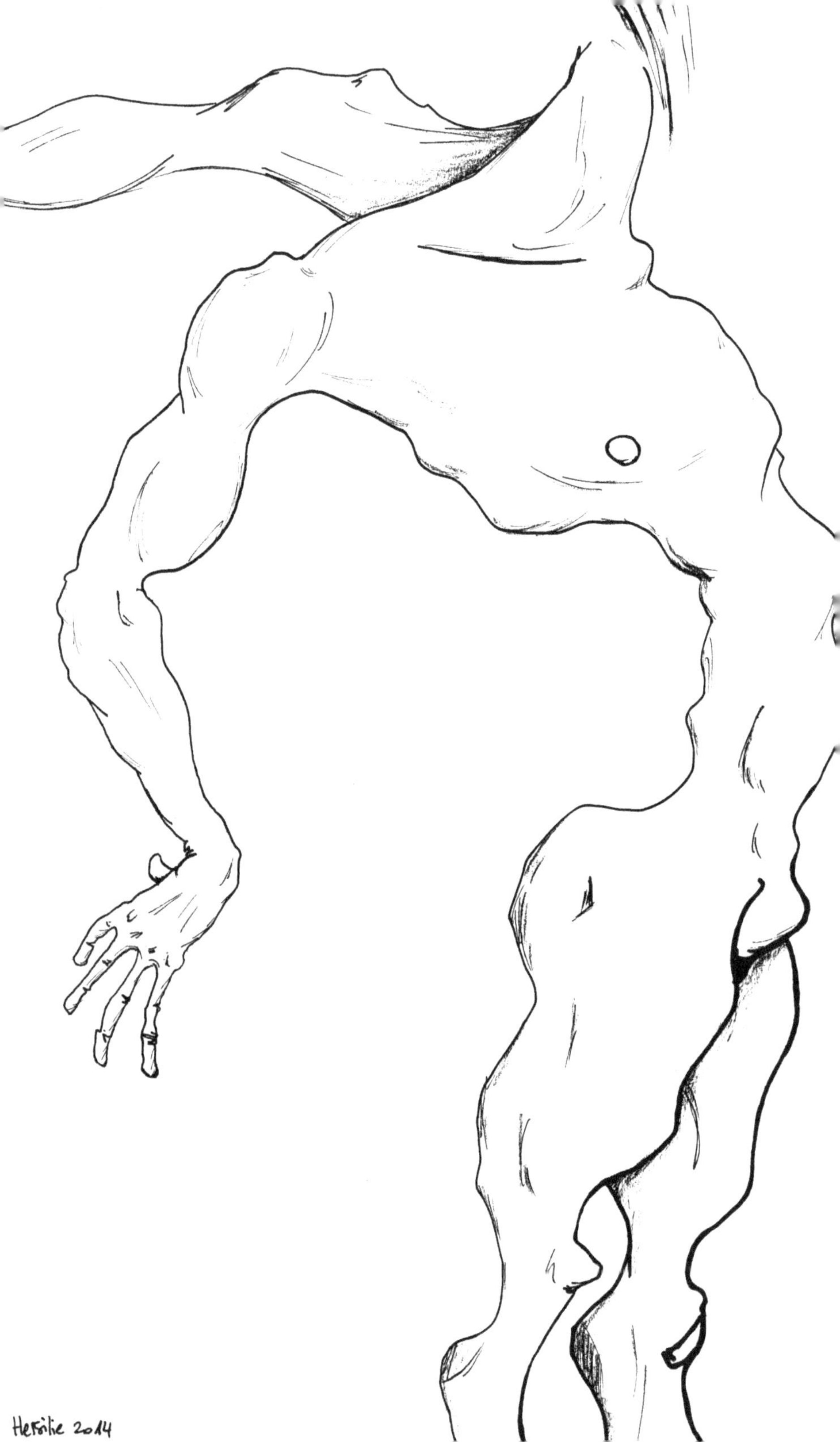
Hersilie 2014

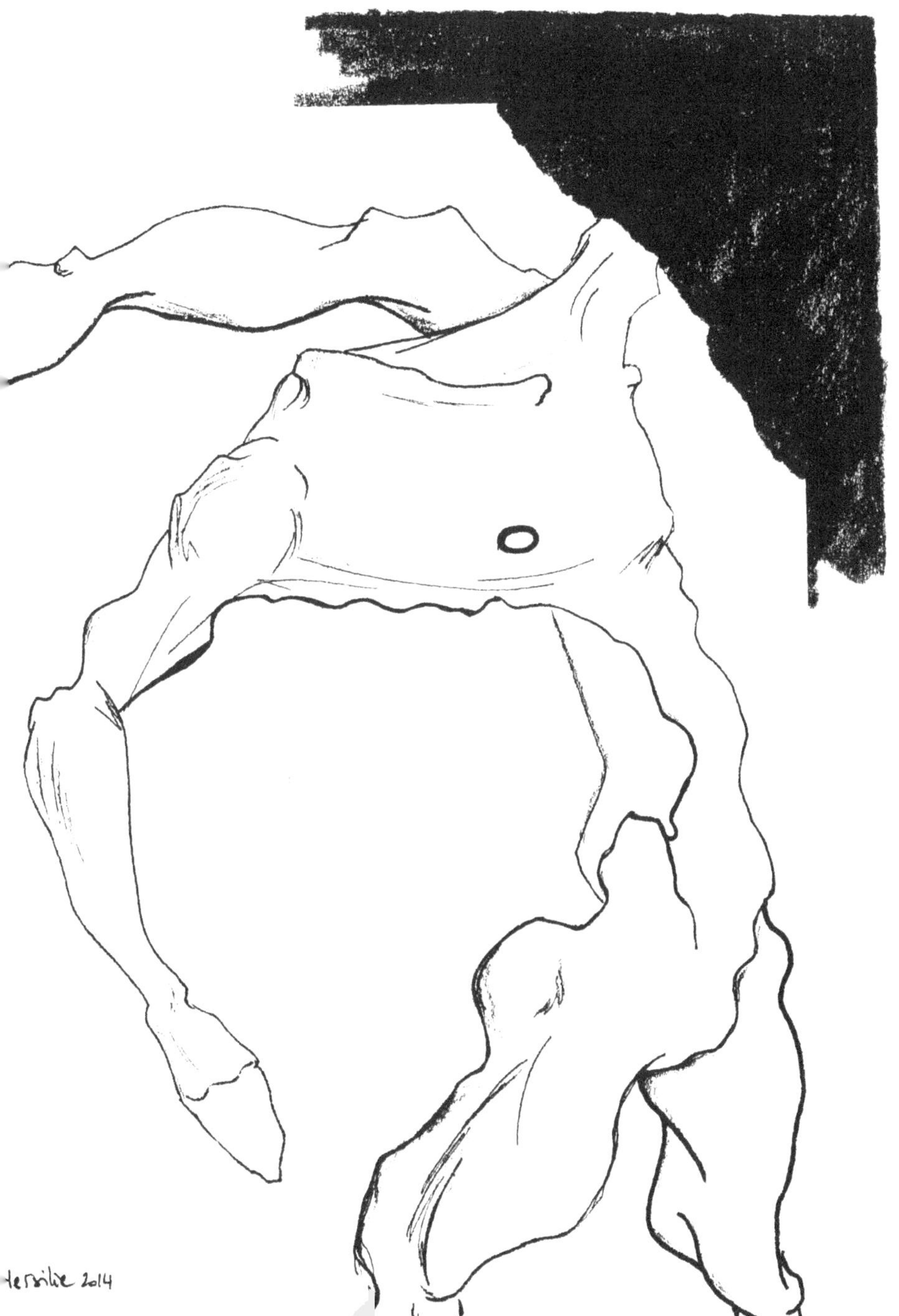
ersilie 2014

Veranda millimetrica

Chi ha infranto la tregua?

Lo chiedono incessanti
a finte civette plastiche
bambini che vagano sperduti
nella notte, con piccole torce in mano
su una veranda millimetrica.

Guardano, guardano, guardano
qualcosa nel buio
                    (...e che arde)
poi si stringono contro un muro
tutto d'invenzione.

Nessuno sa chi per primo ha infranto la tregua.
Nessuno sa da dove vengono i bambini
dove hanno attraversato la frontiera—
                    da quale grembo,
da quale pugno.

Nessuno conosce la data.

Loro si limitano alla conta dei millimetri
                    di pioggia
e a vagare a grandi passi
                    sulla veranda che affonda.

The Millimetric Porch

Who broke the ceasefire?

Children wandering at night
with a small torch
ask this question endlessly
of plastic owls
down on a porch measured in millimetres

They gaze, gaze and gaze again
at something in the dark
                    (…it blazes)
sticking to a wall
of invention.

Nobody knows who broke the ceasefire first.
Nobody knows where the children came from
where they crossed the frontier—
                    whose the womb,
whose the fist.

Nobody knows the day.

They just count the millimeters
                    of rain
swirling round
                    the drowning porch.

Lorenzo Mari

Make Love Not War

"Make love not war," my daddy said. Alla time he said it. Like when we was watchin tv and the news showed bombs hittin houses in far away places and you could see the crossed hairs of the fighter plane's sights and then the target was a cloud of dust like in them roadrunner cartoons, and my daddy would say then to anyone as would listen, "Make love not war."

'Course, my daddy was made imperfect, like most daddys is, and he'd say one thing and plum do another. Make love not war—'cept this one time I recall and I reckon he done both at the same time. My mama heard as how he was makin love with Julie-two-cents down the road, every Friday night after work. They calls her 'two-cents' cos she ain't all there in her head and my daddy was takin advantage, my mama said. Mama spittin wasps by then and lookin for a war, and my daddy gave as good as he got when they was fightin.

Then me and Kev was playin one day. I remember it though it was way back. My daddy said I was knee high to a grasshopper in them days and he called me lil' britches, like that bear done with that kid in the jungle film. And me and Kev, we had these plastic guns and green plastic helmets, like we was soldiers in a battle. And right in the middle I remembers what my daddy was allus sayin and I stopped firin and I stood close to Kev and closer. And I kissed him like he was a girl.

That started a whole lot of other fightin, 'tween Kev's daddy and my daddy, and I was not to play with Kev after that. We got past it eventually and high school overtook us and we didn't mention that kiss to no one, not ever. And Kev was with a girl called May and I was with a girl called Freda, only my daddy kept calling her 'freedom', which pissed me off and pissed Freda off, too. And the years just got up and ran away from us.

Then I heard as how Kev had signed up, you know, and I felt kinda sad. I took him out for a drink one night, when he'd got a letter to say where and when he was to be deployed. We swore a lot and he kept punchin my arm and spittin in the street and sayin "fuck" like he couldn't believe it, any of it. And it was at the dark end of the night, and we was walkin home and walkin the long way cos we wasn't walkin straight, and we was maybe a lil' drunk or a lot drunk, and I said to Kev how I remembered that kiss when we was boys.

He laughed and he said he remembered the war afterwards, his daddy and my daddy givin it big talk and their words all punchin and kickin. Then we was all quiet, me and Kev, and a little awkward, and I put my hands in my pockets to stop myself reachin out for him, reachin out for Kev who was goin off to be a real fuckin soldier in two days. And Kev, I noticed, did the same with his hands and his pockets, and like that we left it.

Kev's mama reads his letters out to the whole street when they come. All the kids and the women. I stand as close as I dare and I listen to see what he's got to say and to see if he mentions me in his letters, but mostly just to know that he's safe.

Lindsay Fisher

Petit pouce gisant
(en amas) sous terre. Pris d'assaut
à la peine de tous.

Chloé Jouanne

about the contributors

Oliver James Lomax is a thirty year old artist, poet, and lyricist from Bolton. He lives, works, and records in Liverpool and Manchester. He has exhibited across Europe and the UK, reading at gallerys and poetry events. Last year he contributed his poem 'England's New Trinity of Love' to the *Morning Star's* 'We are all in this Together' Protest record. He is signed to the label Cityscape Records, his work is available to listen to and download from their website.

Tim Quinlan is a Dublin-based writer and teacher. He has been writing poetry for more than 30 years in both Irish and English and recently published his first Irish-language collection *Aistear Anama* with the Onslaught Press.

Anna Husain is an award-winning poet who has been published in several anthologies, newspapers, and chapbooks. She was a featured poet in the Lifestyles section of the *Chicago Tribune*, has had her own local Arts & Letters page, and been a featured poet at Bucktown Arts Fest (Chicago, IL), while maintaining membership in several poetry organizations. Anna has been writing for over twenty years.

Rethabile Masilo is a Mosotho poet who enjoys reading and writing. He lives in Paris with his wife and two children. Rethabile is self-employed and works in language-teaching. He says he has been writing for a good while, learning through trial and error and picking up lots of sounds by reading and re-reading the poems that he likes. His work has been published in various magazines and online.

Born in 1961 in Lesotho, he left his country with his parents and siblings to go into exile in 1980. He moved through the Republic of South Africa (a very short stay, on account of the weight of Apartheid), Kenya, and The United States of America, before settling in France in 1987.

He blogs at *Poéfrika* and co-edits with Phil Rice the literary magazine *Canopic Jar*.

Dave Rendle is just an individual based in Cardigan, West Wales, a Welsh speaker currently without work, but committed to the the ethos of solidarity and freedom. He strongly supports the cause of the Palestinian people. He is a member of a group of local poets who, once a month, meet and perform under the name 'The Cellar Bards'. He is actively involved in his local Amnesty International Group, and is a keen blogger, under the name 'teifidancer'.

Mathew D. Staunton: Originally from Coolock in Dublin, Mathew is a historian, teacher, and printmaker. He divides his time between having fun with his daughter, Aoife, research, teaching, making books, and printing on a small press at the bottom of his garden. He also edits and illustrates for Everytpe in Mayo and runs The Onslaught Press in Oxford.

Colm Herron's first writing career began at the age of seven when he stitched together his vampire stories on his big sister's Singer sewing machine and sold them to classmates for a penny a piece. He was in business. Two years later he was telling cliff-hangers to the ne'er-do-wells in the local gambling hall. When he was fifteen he had a play on BBC and later brought his short stories to Brian Friel, an emerging playwright. Friel said "Great. This stuff's better than what I wrote at your age.' But Colm was unimpressed and thought "This guy's going nowhere. I don't know why I came to him at all." So Colm gave up writing, deciding to live instead. Meanwhile Friel took off and, while his plays were showing worldwide for the next thirty years,stories were kicking and turning in Colm's head. But they still weren't ready to come out. Till twelve years ago, that is, when he said to himself "OK, I've lived. Maybe it's time to do the other thing." Thus began his second writing career. And his latest novel The Wake (And What Jeremiah Did Next) will be released later this year by publishers Nuascéalta Teoranta.

Michael Rosen is an award-winning children's writer and poet, and the author of more than 140 books. He was the fifth British Children's Laureate and has recently been appointed Professor of Children's Literature at Goldsmiths, University of London

Jamaican-Canadian Pamela Mordecai writes plays, poems, and stories for children and adults. Her poetry collections include *Journey Poem*, *de Man: a performance poem*, *Certifiable*, *The True Blue of Islands* and *Subversive Sonnets*. *Pink Icing* is a collection of short fiction. She and her husband Martin wrote *Culture and Customs of Jamaica*, a reference work. Dundurn Press will publish her first novel, *Cipher*, in spring 2015. She lives in Ontario, Canada.

Andrea Brady was born in Philadelphia and studied at Columbia University and Cambridge. She is a poet and has performed throughout the UK, Europe, Canada, and the US. She has been invited to speak as an expert by the British Council, the BBC, the Arts Council, and the Poetry Society. Her work has been translated into French, German, Spanish, Slovene, Slovak, and Finnish.

Steve Pottinger is a performance poet who gigs whenever and wherever he can. His work has been published in the *Morning Star*, and on *Poetry24*, and his fourth volume of poems will be out later this year. He has a website at stevepottinger.co.uk

Sally Flint's poetry has been widely published and anthologized. She teaches creative writing, facilitates community workshops and is co-founder/editor of *Riptide* short story journal and Canto Poetry at the University of Exeter. She is currently working with young people from The Amber Foundation on producing a series of poems inspired by images from WWI. Her research interests include healthcare in the arts, and the relationship between poetry, visual art and technology. Her collection *Pieces of Us* is now available www.worplepress.com

Moe Seager is a writer and performance artist. A Poet and Jazz & Blues vocalist, he sings his verses on stages in Paris, New York, and elsewhere. He has recorded two jazz-poetry CDs with the Blue Note Metaphor. His poetry collections are *Rio Escondido* (French Ministry of Culture), *One World* (Cairo press, in Arabic translation), *We want Everything*, (les Temps des Cerises, Paris, in French translation), and *Fishermen and Pool Sharks* (Busking editions, London). His essays have been broadcast on radio, television, in print, and online as Paris Calling. Seager has had numerous works performed, commissioned for stages in the USA and France. A Golden Quill Awardee, 1989, (USA) for journalism, Seager earned an International Human Rights award, 1990, from the Zepp foundation, for his numerous features, essays and poems for radio, print, online, written on site from numerous war zones in Central America, Middle East, Africa, Detroit. Seager lives in voluntary exile in Paris.

Rustum Kozain is a South African poet living in Cape Town. He has published two collections of poetry, *This Carting Life* and *Groundwork*.

Michel Jovet practices escape from everyday life near Paris, France through writing, recording songs that, sometimes, he has written, listening to a lot of metal and watching a lot of horror movies. All of this with a little help from his friends.

Dr Radha Valaulikar is a 25-year old medical doctor from the state of Goa, India. She specializes in Community Medicine and believes that every individual in this world must have access to at least the basic health care services. She condemns war of any kind, fought for any reason that may take a toll on the lives of innocent citizens who are at no fault as well as on the resources of a country that can be put to better use in so many areas.

Ru Freeman's creative and political writing has appeared internationally. She is the author of the novels *A Disobedient Girl* (Atria/Simon & Schuster, 2009) and *On Sal Mal Lane* (Graywolf, 2013), a New York Times Editor's Choice. Both novels have been translated into several languages including Italian, French, Hebrew, and Chinese. She blogs for the *Huffington Post* on literature and politics, is a contributing editorial board member of the *Asian American Literary Review*, and has been a fellow of the Bread Loaf Writers' Conference, Yaddo and the Virginia Center for the Creative Arts.

Nazle Arbee is a 19-year old poet and student of anthropology from South Africa.

Neil Young hails from Belfast and now lives in north-east Scotland. He blames his addiction to poetry on hanging round public libraries too much as a teen. Described by Brian Patten as "a socialist poet par excellence", he is a regular reader at poetry venues, on radio and at festivals. His first book, Lagan Voices, a Belfast memoir, was published by Scryfa in 2011. He is co-founder of a new forum/magazine, *The Poets' Republic*, and organiser and host of a series of war poetry readings under the banner of 'No Glory'.

Steve Willey lives in Whitechapel. His poetry has been anthologized in *Dear World and Everyone In It* (Bloodaxe, 2013) and *Better Than Language* (Ganzfeld press, 2011). His long-form poem *Elegy* was published by Veer Books (December 2013). In August 2013 Steve travelled to Palestine with a grant from the International Artists Award (funded by British Council and Arts Council England) to develop his long-form poem *Living In*, which he began when visiting the West Bank in 2009. Throughout August 2014 he will be the Writer In Residence at the The University of Arizona Poetry Center

Rebecca Tamás was born in London and studied at the University of Warwick and at the University of Edinburgh, where she won the Grierson Verse Prize. Her poems have been published in a variety of magazines and journals including Magma, Oxford Poetry and The SHOp. Her first poetry collection, *The Ophelia Letters* was published by Salt in 2013.

Nuala Herron: I've always been interested in painting the human form, whether it's the entire figure or just the face. I have also painted more abstract pieces including cityscapes and dilapidated buildings. But ultimately, what I think every artist finds the most difficult and challenging, is representing the human form realistically. For this reason, I've always been more interested in representational painting rather than abstract. I find it more satisfying to spend months on a painting and try to improve each time. I love painting people and telling a story through paint. Although I started out painting from life, I now work from photographs as it's more practical and can sometimes give me more freedom.

'The Pipeline' shows two children, hand in hand, walking across a pipeline in an oppressed country. This is a simple, and I hope, effective image.

I am an award-winning artist from Derry, Northern Ireland and I've exhibited locally and internationally.

Vanessa Gebbie is a Welsh writer living in England. She is a novelist (*The Coward's Tale*, Bloomsbury), short story writer (*Words from a Glass Bubble* and *Storm Warning: Echoes of Conflict*, Salt) and poet *(The Half-life of Fathers*, Pighog). Recipient of an Arts Council Grant for the Arts, she is contributing editor of *Short Circuit: Guide to the Art of the Short Story*, editions 1 and 2 (Salt), has been awarded a Hawthornden Fellowship and residencies at both Gladstone's Library and Stockholm University. www.vanessagebbie.com

Alison Bown is a sound designer, writer and educator with credits on feature films, games, TV and short form animation. Born in Leeds, Yorkshire, Alison worked as a musician and participatory media producer before attended the National Film and Television School to study Sound Post Production. After a stint on Harry Potter for Electronic Arts, Alison worked in Soho for Paul Davies Sound Design before leaving for Bristol where she is now finishing her first novel.

Alison read English Lit and Drama at Loughborough University and has been developing her writing for the last ten years. Her novel has received support and interest from both established writers and agents and this has considerably cheered on the long process of writing it. She is also a consultant in Creative Industries education, leading nationally on Creative and Digital Media Apprenticeships to diversify entry routes for new talent

Cristiana Ziraldo is a teacher of English as a Foreign Language and a teacher of Literatures in English at a high-school in Pordenone, Italy. She teaches creative writing to all those students who wish to unbridle their imagination. She is also a teacher trainer. She deeply believes in the power of poetry and in the power of reading to make young people envisage a better world.

Roz Goddard co-ordinates the West Midlands Readers' Network, an organisation that works extensively with libraries and readers' groups, produces reading events and commissions new work from regional writers. She is also a poet and short-fiction writer. She has published four collections of poems, the most recent *The Sopranos Sonnets and other poems* (Nine Arches Press) featured on R3's The Verb and her work is on permanent display in Birmingham Museum and Art Gallery. She is currently working on a new collection of poems. Examples of her poetry and fiction can be found here: www.rozgoddard.com.

AE Ballakisten is a poet and social philosopher who lived under Apartheid in South Africa for the first 24 years of his life. He has published two volumes of poetry and a children's book. He holds Masters degrees from Harvard, M.I.T. and the University of London.

Romain Renault studied Fine Art and Animation at Rennes, Poitiers and ENSAD, Paris in France. Nowadays, he navigates the field of digital creation with the making of video-games and digital animation for for others and for himself... he also wants to stay connected to a more traditional creation, with the use of good old pencils and paintbrushes on paper and canvas to keep the energy flowing! He chose to be part of the book because when he sees human rights flouted by dogmas, he is ashamed of human absurdity.

Soraya Hamlaoui is a Paris-based multi-disciplinary visual artist who works with sculpture, installation, performance and drawing. She studied interior architecture in Lyon and graduated from ENSAD, Paris in 2012. Most of her projects question the relationship between appearance and reality

John Staunton is undead and living in Dublin. He has written and produced many plays, dozens of short stories, and a plethora of poetry. He remains unimpressed and feels overly under-appreciated.

Pat Jourdan went to Liverpool College of Art and also writes poetry, stories and novels. Her latest short story collection, *The Fog Index* was launched at the International Short Story Conference in Vienna. After many years in Ireland, she lives down a country lane in Suffolk, with seagulls often on the chimney.

Roland Singer-Kingsmith studied Arabic and Islamic Studies at Oxford University. Since graduating in 2011 he has worked in the Middle East for international development agencies including the British Council. He visited Palestine for the first time in April 2013 as part of a youth delegation in order to meet with leading figures of civil society in the West Bank. This trip, more than anything else, has shaped his views about the injustice of the occupation and the settlement programme and he is now an active member of the Palestine Solidarity Campaign and the Boycott, Divestment and Sanctions movement in the UK. He keeps a blog about occupation in Palestine (http://non-violent-vigilante.tumblr.com).

Maggie Harris is a Guyanese poet and prose writer living in the UK. Her first collection of Poetry, *Limbolands*, won the Guyana Prize for Literature 2000. She is this year's (2014) Caribbean Regional Winner of the Commonwealth Short Story Prize. Her memoir, *Kiskadee Girl*, is published by Kingston University Press, her short stories by Cultured Llama Press and her recent poetry by Cane Arrow Press. www.maggieharris.co.uk.

Ilhan Tahir is a Turkish Cypriot born and raised in London. He graduated from Brunel University in 2012 with a BA in English with Creative Writing. He has always been passionate about Palestine as he feels the suffering taking place there is one of the greatest failures of modern day society, and with the incredible amount of apathy to the Palestinians plight shown by Western media, he feels it is important to at least make his voice heard.

Hersilie Derrien studied illustration at the HKu in Utrecht and is currently based in Paris where she paints and is obsessed with anatomy.

Lorenzo Mari lives and works in Bologna,Italy. He has authored four collections of poetry; the latest one is entitled *Nel debito di affiliazione* (In the affiliation's debt, L'Arcolaio, 2013). He translates from English and Spanish into Italian. Recently, he has collaborated with the intercultural theatre group Cantieri Meticci, based in Bologna.

Lindsay Fisher leaks stories. It is an age thing, they say. It can't be helped. Sometimes they pool in the dirt and dry to nothing; sometimes they spill into nice places, and people say stuff about the stories. Currently work appears in *Stories For Homes*, an anthology sold in aid of Shelter, a UK based charity for the homeless; and in *Cease Cows* a new online literary magazine; and several pieces are available published at Ether Books and online at 1000 words.

Chloé Jouanne is a Paris-based journalism student with roots in Iowa and a fierce sense of justice.

www.ingramcontent.com/pod-product-compliance
Lightning Source LLC
LaVergne TN
LVHW052251100826
845147LV00001B/12

9780992723842